THE COMPTON COWBOYS

THE

COMPTON COWBOYS

THE NEW GENERATION OF COWBOYS IN AMERICA'S URBAN HEARTLAND

WALTER THOMPSON-HERNÁNDEZ

WITHDRAWN

wm

WILLIAM MORROW
An Imprint of HarperCollins*Publishers*

FIRST EDITION

Designed by Bonni Leon-Berman

All photographs are courtesy of the author unless otherwise credited

Library of Congress Cataloging-in-Publication Data has been applied for.

ISBN 978-0-06-291060-8

20 21 22 23 24 LSC 10 9 8 7 6 5 4 3 2 1

for my mama, Eleuteria Hernández González

when the lights shine off

and it's my turn to settle down,

my main concern,

promise that you will sing about me,

promise that you will sing about me.

—*KENDRICK LAMAR*

CONTENTS

THE COMPTON COWBOYS

PROLOGUE

I ALWAYS WONDERED WHY I never learned about black cowboys in any of my elementary school classes in Huntington Park, a city in Southeast Los Angeles. The only cowboys we learned about were white. We were taught that they rode through trails, herded cattle, and occasionally got into gunfights with bandits and Native Americans. Even Mrs. Sanders, a black woman and my favorite teacher, never once mentioned black cowboys. The history of the West until that point had appeared exclusively white. Little did I know there were groups in nearby Compton who were actively trying to reinsert black cowboys into the history books.

But something always seemed a bit off. It felt like we were celebrating the lives of men who had often terrorized their way through native communities in the West. Cowboys, I would later learn, were white men who rode through towns with reckless abandon and left a trail of destruction behind them. None of it sat well with me. I was the type of kid who chose to disrupt our annual schoolwide Thanksgiving celebration in the third grade by jumping on a table and yelling that Christopher Columbus was a "murderer" and killed thousands of indigenous people throughout the Americas. The incident landed me a two-week suspension but an emphatic high-five from my then twenty-six-year-old mother, who was active in many social justice circles as a Ph.D. student in literature at the University of California, Los Angeles.

All this added up to real confusion when I first learned about the black cowboys in Compton. I was six, and my mama and I were driving to the Compton Swap Meet one Saturday afternoon. When she wasn't reading or writing or completing her coursework, Mama worked as a valet parking attendant at a fancy hotel in Santa Monica. As a result, I spent lots of time with my aunts, who worked close to our home. Weekends were sometimes the only time when my mama and I got to see one another.

It was 1991 and we were living in a three-bedroom home that we shared with my grandmother, two aunts, uncle, and two cousins. If you lived in our neighborhood, chances were the Chicano rapper Kid Frost's hit song "La Raza" was playing loudly on someone's boombox or car speakers. If you lived in Watts or Compton, located about ten minutes away, you were more likely to hear an N.W.A record like "Express Yourself" or the soulful sounds of Teddy Pendergrass coming from an old head's flashy Cadillac.

Back then, South Central and the city of Compton were in complete upheaval. Gang violence often led to high murder rates, the crack cocaine epidemic was destroying families, and rising unemployment rates were forcing black families to leave the area en masse in search of jobs and affordable housing in cities outside of Los Angeles. At the same time, Mexican immigrants fleeing dwindling economic markets in Mexico were slowly migrating to the same communities that black folks were leaving, which sometimes caused racial tensions. Black folks often blamed Mexican immigrants for stealing jobs and taking over their neighborhoods, while Mexicans—who sometimes arrived in these neighborhoods with their own preconceived ideas about blackness—often scorned their black neighbors for not working hard. Both stereotypes were rooted in deep misunderstandings and false images projected by the media.

Whenever my mama and I drove to Compton, she would instruct me to lock our doors and make sure our windows were sealed shut as we drove across the train tracks on Alameda Street that served as a natural border between the brown community that I lived in and the black one we were driving into. Carjackings were frequent in those days and several of my relatives had been victims of different forms of robbery over the years, prompting my mama to drive with caution.

As I grew older, though, I realized that the precautions she took were often driven by deeper issues. Some of the very people whom I would call my friends and family held on to their own racist ideas about black people. *Mayates,* a derogatory Spanish term used to describe people of African descent, was one of the first words I ever heard referring to black people. I was receiving a message that black folks were dangerous and prone to violence, but, nevertheless, I felt a strong connection to Compton.

As the son of an African-American father whom I didn't really meet until my early twenties, hearing these slurs directed at black people forced me to reckon with the idea that a part of my heritage could be supported while the other parts could be weaponized. I had no contact with my father and thus no contact with my black family. This made our drives to Compton more complicated than they appeared to be. I was being taught that black people were dangerous, which made me believe that I, in fact, was dangerous, but our drives also gave me the chance to dream: every time we drove to Compton, I naively believed that I might serendipitously run into my father or another black relative. My worldview was small and limited, and in my mind, Compton was the only place where black folks lived. I looked out of our car window as we drove south on Long Beach Boulevard past Martin Luther King Jr. Boulevard and under the 105

Freeway overpass and didn't see the criminals that people in my community talked about. Instead, I saw my family.

During some of our weekend drives, I'd see Compton's black cowboys at various intersections. Sometimes I'd see them riding their horses along the train tracks on Alameda Street that transported goods from the shipping docks in Long Beach to downtown Los Angeles warehouses, and vice versa. "Look at the black cowboys, *mijo*," Mama would say as she stared in awe while waving at them on the street. I'd look at them and naively ask myself, "Are the men on these horses my family?"

We weren't alone in our fascination. The cowboys were showstoppers. Cars would honk and drivers would wave in admiration as they trotted past. Their only competition were the classic car clubs that cruised the same streets every weekend in 1964 Chevrolet Impalas or El Camino Super Sports.

The cowboys had an allure to them that went beyond words. They seemed ethereal—like superheroes on the backs of mystic creatures who, I imagined, communicated in a language unknown to me. These men were different from the canonical "classic" cowboy—the white men I'd seen on television in Clint Eastwood films or in Marlboro advertisements somewhere in the West with cigarettes in their mouths. The only other image of cowboys that I had seen was the Mexican men who rode horses and worked on ranches in my mother's hometown of Magdalena, a small rural town full of *rancheros* in the state of Jalisco. Seeing black cowboys riding through an urban neighborhood like Compton was incredibly transformative. It went against every conventional idea that I had at the time. These weren't the cowboys I had learned about in my history books or seen on the big screen, and yet as I watched them ride at dusk on the same back streets known for rappers like Eazy-E and Dr. Dre, I recognized something inherent in the cowboys who existed in every western film and every hip-hop song: these black men were nonconformist, independent, and strong. They commanded attention and embodied a rebellious spirit, and, most importantly, they were utterly inspiring.

Years later, as a *New York Times* reporter, I reached out to a group of young black men who were calling themselves the Compton Cowboys. This group, like their predecessors, continued to ride horses through the city's streets with a free and rebellious spirit. All of them learned how to ride on a ranch in the middle of Compton's Richland Farms. This group, however, was doing more than riding horses for recreation. They were riding horses to free themselves from some of the dangers of street and gang life and as a way to heal from the trauma that haunted their lives. Their motto said it all: "Streets raised us. Horses saved us." I wanted to learn more.

THE PARADE

WITH STRONG LOW-PRESSURE SYSTEMS COMING from the west, local weather forecasters predicted what the horses on the ranch had already sensed: one of the largest storms of the year was on the horizon and heading directly toward the farms. On any other weekend, rain wouldn't have been an issue. California was withering under a five-year drought. But the weekend of the 65th annual Compton Christmas Parade, rain couldn't have come at a more inopportune time.

The parade was the pride and joy of an embattled city. Decades of economic neglect and a host of corruption scandals involving moot energy schemes, faulty city contracts, and the disbandment of the Compton Police Department had left their mark. Until Aja Brown, the city's second female mayor and its youngest, was elected in 2013, the parade was only a shadow of its former self.

But Brown's election ushered in a resurgence of hope in a city with one of the highest death-by-gun rates in the country, bringing prominent Compton natives like rapper Kendrick Lamar to ride as its grand marshal. Canceling the parade would squander months of meticulous planning and tireless fund-raising by teams of diligent organizers. Above all, it would have robbed the joy from families like the Johnsons—one of the many African-American families who had been priced out of their Compton home in the early 1990s but continued to drive back to see the parade every year, in the Johnsons' case from Las Vegas.

Several of the horses began feeling restless hours before the first grey clouds started to form over the city. They neighed loudly and flapped their long, coarse tails, prompting a cacophony of sounds from other horses in nearby ranches throughout the farms. When the clouds finally did appear, they moved in like sentient beings, eerily aware of the potential they had to alter thousands of weekend plans. The rain started as a light, soft drizzle, growing into a heavy downpour within an hour. Local drainage canals, deteriorating from years of physical neglect, got hit the hardest. They immediately overflowed with the city's garbage as the rushing current headed south toward the Los Angeles River and the Pacific Ocean.

After listening to a Spanish radio weather announcement earlier that day, Mr. Sanchez made sure to pack his large blue tarp onto his pickup truck after loading it with fresh meat, tortillas, and an assortment of vegetables he had bought from the market earlier that day. He always had the fewest clients whenever it rained, and not having a protective covering over his stall drastically affected business.

But when the water began to pour through the tarp and onto the tables and chairs, he knew it was time to pack up his one-man taco stand and head home for the night. "That's it for tonight, amigo," he said to Jerome Jordan, a sixty-five-year-old black man who had worked for him for the past two years directing cars into a nearby abandoned lot in exchange for a few dollars and a plate of *al pastor* tacos at the end of each night. Like others his age, Jerome had lived through both the 1965 Watts riots and the 1992 Los Angeles riots. He had seen his city go through changes that, as the years passed, his fading memory was beginning to lose track of.

"God is mad at us tonight," Mr. Sanchez said as the two friends looked up at the heavens with astonishment.

A few blocks away, at the intersection of Tamarind and Alon-dra, in front of the social services building, red streetlights affected by a short circuit flashed continuously, forcing drivers to take turns as they cautiously drove across the intersection while a thick layer of fog crept into the city.

The rain fell hard on the city's homes that night. Midcentury architecture not made for heavy storms meant leaks. Buckets were lined up in the middle of living rooms and bedrooms throughout the city. As the downpour continued, the smell of freshly released petrichor from local flower gardens filled the night air with the scent of an open-air flower shop on a spring day. The delicate aroma gave people like Diego, a middle-aged homeless man from Mexico City, who had worked at a flower market in his early twenties, a chance to momentarily revel in the memories of his youth. The aroma drifted into his makeshift tent, reminding him of the flowers he once abandoned for the promise that lay on the other side of the border more than thirty years ago. He held tightly to a beer can the entire night next to other brown men who had been lured by the same dream. His was the only mouth that formed a smile.

Back on the ranch, the rain continued to fall on the weary tin roofs that protected the horses from the elements. Puddles of cold, muddy water collected in each stall, creating the perfect conditions for the spread of thrush, a fungus that threatened horse hooves.

Helio, one of the largest black Thoroughbreds on the ranch, neighed the loudest and moved erratically in his stall. Chocolate, a black elder Canadian pony, rolled around in the mud, making his coat two shades darker with every turn. Sonny, one of the other quarter horses, aggressively chewed on the metal gate that separated him from Fury. On the opposite side of the ranch, Red

Dog, an Australian cattle dog who protected the property and frequently barked at the horses, scurried into the barn for protection, where he spent the rest of the night curled up next to a barrel of hay.

BYRON HOOK BEGAN feeling antsy as he tossed and turned inside his brown-carpeted bedroom. The rain had stopped in the middle of the night, and by morning the sun had crept out. Byron was five feet ten inches tall and weighed close to 240 pounds, and his brown wooden single bed creaked loudly every time he turned his body in a different direction. The only thing louder was the sound of the Gutierrez family's crowing rooster next door, which signaled his internal clock that it was time to wake up for his first cigarette of the day.

Usually the first one awake on the ranch, Byron was also the earliest to bed, usually after watching the same cowboy westerns that he used to watch with his parents as a child in nearby Harbor City. One of the last remaining original gangsters on the block, he had lived to see the Richland Farms go through many of its transformations. Like the oak and sycamore trees that proudly lined both sides of the streets, he had seen more than he had ever needed to.

Back in the late 1980s, when the farms were predominantly African-American, Byron was known around the neighborhood for his flashy customized lowrider bike. Its long, curved banana seat and tall upward-curving silver-chromed handlebars nobly glistened under the Compton sun, highlighting the shiny blue paint that adorned its sides. At one point he had attached a homemade speaker system to the back of his bike and played the same CDs that he burned and sold for a profit at local swap meets and lowrider car shows.

In those days, five dollars could get you an entire album, ten dollars could get you three, and twenty could get you five. It was how Byron made his money, supported his drug fix, and made friends in the neighborhood. If his nephews, Randy and Carlton, were lucky, he'd let them stand on his back pegs and hang on to his shoulders while he rode up and down Caldwell Street.

At fifty-six, though, Byron had become only a shadow of that proud young man. Several operations on a left arm that had a birth defect, and encroaching symptoms of dementia, had left his body badly weakened. Streaming music services like Spotify had wiped out his music scheme. With almost no other way to make money, he began to panhandle around the neighborhood, sometimes coming home with a few dollars in his pockets, sometimes with nothing. Whenever his change requests hit a dry spell and his monthly Social Security checks ran low, he reverted to more drastic measures, choosing to walk around the farms checking for unlocked car doors hoping to find whatever he could get his hands on inside.

The cigarette filter burned as he rocked back and forth on the porch chair while attempting to stay warm inside his blue long-sleeved T-shirt. The left side of his greying hair lay flattened while his right side puffed out of his head. Everyone on the ranch knew which side Byron slept on by which side of his hair was flat the next morning. Only his bushy salt-and-pepper eyebrows looked even.

After taking a long puff of the Newport cigarette that he had been nursing for the past thirty minutes, Byron murmured a series of indistinguishable words that only he could understand. At this point in his life, his speech, much like his body, had slowed and was worsening by the day.

The front screen door flew open, barely missing the side of his face. "What up, Byron?" his nephew Carlton asked. He was wearing a pair of black sweats, sandals with white socks, and a white snug-fitting tank top, completely unaware that he had nearly hit his uncle's face.

Carlton sat down on the porch steps, protected from the sun by the roof overhead. His dreads hung free, just out of the view of his glasses, but low enough to graze the "C" and "H" tattoos on his wiry shoulders that Keenan Abercrombia had done in his backyard a few years earlier.

"You-you . . . almost gah-gah-gah damn hi-hi-hit me mothafucka," Byron said with a deep stammer, struggling to get every word out.

"Man, what you talking about?" Carlton quickly responded, looking back at his uncle in bewilderment. "You trippin'."

Like Byron, Carlton had a morning routine that never wavered. His was called wake and bake: a ceremonial activity that involved smoking a marijuana-filled cigar called a backwood as soon as he woke up in the morning. Wake and bake was as routine to Carlton as brushing his teeth or eating breakfast. Not smoking in the mornings affected his mood for the entire day, and his ability to function.

"Aye, you got a lighter?" he quietly asked Byron. In his left hand was a half-smoked 'wood that he had saved from the previous night. He held a cracked-screen iPhone in his other hand that pulsed quick-paced southern melodic trap music.

Carlton's voice rarely ever rose beyond a low murmur. As a younger twin, he deferred to his brother, Randy. He was quiet and reserved and preferred the sound of others' voices over his own.

"Man, you always t-t-t-taking my gah, gah, damn lighter," Byron aggressively responded. "I just got t-t-t-this one. Why you always—t-t-t-trying to steal my shit?"

Lighters were hard to come by on the farms and too expensive to replace regularly. The last time Byron let Carlton borrow his, he'd never returned it.

Carlton repeated his question again, this time with an outstretched hand, still looking down at his phone, unfazed by his uncle's emotional plea. Down the street near the intersection of Center and Caldwell, horses' hooves loudly pounded the asphalt while the two continued their exchange.

"Here," a dejected Byron finally said, pulling out a yellow lighter from inside the pocket of his blue jeans. He knew Carlton was going to keep asking until he got what he wanted.

"But give it ri-right back, you hear?"

"Thanks, man," Carlton said.

Carlton relit his 'wood, took a hit, and released a cloud of fresh smoke into the air as he walked back into the house and into his room, where Young Dolph's "Major" song played from his speakers. He sang it at the top of his lungs.

The twenty-eight-year-old was in good spirits and in the mood to celebrate. He had just gotten paid the night before for his work on the ranch and had spent the entire night with a woman he'd met on Instagram earlier in the week. His work checks didn't amount to more than a few hundred dollars, but they were just enough to spend on weed and the women he met online. Sometimes he saw as many as three or four different women per week.

Despite his small stature, Carlton preferred thicker women who were twice his size, sometimes larger. His love for bigger women had become something of a running joke among the other nine members of the cowboys, but didn't faze a man who had dreams of one day becoming a porn star with the name Horse Dick Carl. The woman he had slept with the night before didn't ask for money, only wanting a meal from McDonald's and an Uber back home. A solid win, Carlton thought to himself as they waited patiently for their Big Macs and apple pies in the drive-thru that night.

He spent the rest of the morning looking through nude photos that women had sent him and scrolling through dating apps, plotting whom he would sleep with next.

WHEN THE CITY of Compton was incorporated in 1888 by founder Griffith D. Compton, it was meant to be a farming town. Approximately thirty pioneering families quickly established a tight-knit community founded on agricultural expertise carried over from the Midwest and the South.

What began as a small, rural town grew as ample residential lots gave families from all over California the chance to raise a family, care for crops, and tend to livestock. The Richland Farms became a ten-acre community in the heart of Compton, blocks away from what would later become the Compton Courthouse and Compton High School and zoned specifically for agricultural use. The farms became a community within a community that allowed families to live a semblance of the lives they once knew.

Rainfall was always welcomed in one of the few remaining agricultural areas in Los Angeles. When most people in the city drove in a hurried frenzy and complained about the rain, residents of the farms celebrated its arrival. Nearly all the current residents came from rural backgrounds in the South and throughout Mexico. Families like the Hooks, one of the last black cowboy families on the farms, had migrated west from Arkansas during the mid-twentieth century as part of the Great Migration, a mass exodus of thousands of black families who settled in cities throughout the northern states and in West Coast hubs like Seattle, San Francisco, Oakland, and Los Angeles.

In Los Angeles, black families from the South arrived with the hope of working in factories newly created by the war. Many of them were drawn to communities like Central Avenue, a mile-long strip that ran north to south, known as the "eastside" of South Los Angeles—one of the few communities in the city where black families were free from covenants that made it illegal for them to own property. Until the mid-1950s, Compton was still predominantly white and unaffordable for most African-Americans. It's where George H. W. Bush, the nation's forty-first president, lived for six months in 1949 with his wife and his son, future president George W. Bush, when he worked at nearby Security Engineering Company.

The closing of factories and plants in the area reduced property prices and triggered white flight, slowly bringing more black families to the "Hub City." Compton's black population rose from 5 percent in 1940 to 40 percent by 1960, and continued to grow as nearby events like the 1965 Watts riots accelerated the rate of white families leaving.

Families like the Hooks chose to live in the farms after moving from nearby Harbor City. It reminded them of the lives that their families had left behind in the South. There were trees, animals, and, most of all, the space to roam and be free. Like other families who moved to Compton in the 1980s, they arrived to a community comprised of black families from various social classes—each of them reaping the benefits of the 1948 U.S. Supreme Court decision that banned racist housing covenants.

Mexican families like the Hooks' next-door neighbors, the Gutierrezes, were also the products of migration. When the Mexican peso was devalued and the North American Free Trade Agreement radically depressed the price of crops in the 1990s, the effects were felt instantly in rural Mexico, destroying the Gutierrez family's livelihood. They too were lured by the promise of work, leaving their pueblo in Jalisco, Mexico, to seek a better life, just as generations of African-Americans had left the South decades before them.

BY MORNING THE rain clouds that had appeared in the sky the night before were replaced by silky cottonlike cumulus clouds that perched above the ranch like watchful bystanders. Rays of sunlight illuminated a pristine blue sky over the Compton Courthouse, backdropped by the snow-peaked San Gabriel Mountains in the distance.

The local forecasters had failed their viewers once again. The rain, which they had said would last all weekend, only stayed around for one night, and the parade would continue as planned. When the Johnsons heard the news at midnight, they packed their things and were already on their second hour of driving en route to Compton by the time the sun came out that morning. As the sun continued to emerge, water dripped from the tin-roofed stables and into each horse stall, creating a mushy blend of dirt and fresh horse droppings. Because resources had been scarce on the ranch in recent years, fixing the holes in each stall had been put off in favor of feeding the animals and paying employees.

The horses were calm now that the storm had passed. Some looked out to the courthouse, while others peered toward Caldwell Street, sending out the occasional baritone neigh and whimsical tail flip. Red Dog was nowhere to be found, probably hiding in someone else's yard or off on one of his three-day hiatuses. Only the roosters continued to crow on schedule.

It was the biggest day of the year on the farms, and the entire city had woken up beaming with anticipation. The Compton, Dominguez, and Centennial High School marching bands and step teams had been practicing for the lead-up to the parade for weeks. In between practicing for their Friday night football games, each school had created new routines that would be revealed at the parade.

Centennial was the heavy favorite, but this year, under the direction of new leadership, Compton High's band and step teams felt confident about their chances as the day approached. Members of each band and teams washed and ironed their uniforms the night before the big parade, eagerly waiting to show the city what they had secretly been working on.

For the Compton Cowboys and other horse riders, the parade had as much to do with pride as it did the need to address safety concerns for riders in the city. The parade was one of the few times of the year where they could ride safely on the streets without the threat of traffic. In recent years, horse and rider deaths had spiked despite pleas by community groups to create more horse lanes near the farms. Speed limits were hardly enforced and loud car music often spooked horses, causing fatal accidents on some of Compton's busiest streets.

During one month in the past five years, the death toll of horses and humans had almost been equal. Still, while the number of horse accidents had picked up, horse riding had become less common and the sight of riders in the streets rarer each year. In the past, as many as five different riding groups rode in the parade, but these days the only two remaining were the Compton

Cowboys and Los Rancheros de Compton, a Mexican group that usually walked away with the award for best equestrian team at the parade each year.

Grooming the horses took up most of the cowboys' time. Keenan, Charles Harris, and Anthony Harris had spent most of the day before the parade washing and brushing their horses in anticipation.

When they arrived to check up on them the following morning, an hour after Byron and Carlton had their first smoke, the ranch was empty. Only Rashid, Mayisha's eldest son, was around. His dreadlocks were covered by a white bandana as he looked over the gate that connected his home to the rest of the ranch. Since moving back over a year before, Rashid had kept out of the way of the cowboys, only showing his face when the smell of weed wafted into his backyard or when he needed to warm his breakfast up at his uncle Louie's house next door.

The 'wood got passed between the three friends. It was a tradition that they had created long after they left Mayisha's Compton Jr. Posse program as teenagers. They were never allowed to smoke weed when she was present, but now that she was around less, they did as they pleased. Horse riding and smoking had almost become a sacred act. One didn't exist without the other. Anthony took a drag and inhaled, puffed out his cheeks, then drew them back in after he released a cloud of smoke.

"Pass that shit over here, nigga," Keenan said while brushing the right side of his horse with a curry comb, using long, broad strokes. He paused and took his time, admiring every stroke on the massive dark brown animal in front of him while continuing to take hits of the 'wood.

Charles's body moved slower than anyone else's that morning. It had been only a couple of hours since he had gotten off the graveyard shift at Walmart. He was running on adrenaline and cold day-old coffee that he had grabbed on his way out of the employee break room.

"I have to go ride some horses," he'd told his manager as he hurried out, patting the outside of the pockets of his pants, looking for his car keys.

"Horses?" his manager asked with a surprised look, hardly believing him.

"Horses!" Charles responded with a smirk before running out of the room.

Keenan was the only one in the group who didn't drive to the ranch that morning. Since his license got suspended earlier that year, Uber had become his transportation of choice when his wife didn't have time to drive him. The young expecting couple shared a two-bedroom apartment in Inglewood just big enough for them and her seven-year-old daughter and within view of the nearby professional football stadium whose construction was further opening the door for gentrification that threatened to raise their rent.

The past few weeks had been particularly challenging for the twenty-seven-year-old. It had been almost a month since he was laid off as a sous-chef in a Louisiana-style restaurant near downtown Los Angeles, and every Uber ride to the ranch put a dent in his dwindling bank account.

"Why you always got the dirtiest horse on the ranch?" Charles asked Carlton, who joined the rest of the guys, still wearing the same clothes he wore earlier that morning.

"Nigga, shut up," Carlton replied. "Why you always on my head?"

"I'm just asking," Charles said with a full grin on his face.

Anthony and Keenan laughed loud enough for the next-door

neighbor's dogs to start barking. They immediately instigated an argument between Carlton and Charles like they had done for the past twenty years. Talking shit was a popular pastime on the ranch. It made time go quicker and it brought everyone together.

"You gonna let him talk to you that way?" Anthony asked, laughing hysterically and grabbing his stomach. "Maaaaaaan . . . I wouldn't!"

Carlton was usually the butt of everyone's jokes and an easy target for Charles, who prided himself on being one of the biggest jokesters on the ranch. There wasn't a day that passed where he didn't find an excuse to clown someone. He made fun of everything. If it walked, he made fun of it. Nothing got past his observant eyes.

At the same time, Charles was also one of the most sensitive cowboys in the group. His jokes often masked the insecurities that he felt; finding pleasure in mocking others deflected from his own shortcomings.

Carlton grabbed Helio, a large black Thoroughbred with long, bushy winter hair, from his stall. He walked him to the gate and tied him up before beginning to brush him. Helio had rolled around in the mud all night, and after a few more brushstrokes, Carlton threw his brush on the ground and walked back to his house without finishing the only duty he had that morning. He had been friends with Charles since they were children and had grown accustomed to his jokes, but it didn't stop him from being annoyed.

"Man, fuck this shit," he said as he left his horse on the gate and slowly walked away, his sweats hanging far below his waist.

"See?" Charles said while looking at Anthony and Keenan. His smile grew wider with every step that Carlton took away from the group. "He soft as hell, man. He softer than a baby's booty!"

An hour passed and the three continued to tend to their horses. It was a practice that they had learned as children and perfected as adults. Being near the stables brought them a sense of peace that began as riders in the Compton Junior Posse, Mayisha's youth riding organization that had brought them all together as children more than twenty years before. They had learned to clean stalls and groom horses before they could ride. But grooming the horses' coats wasn't just to care for the animals; it was also a way to care for themselves. The ranch became a place where they went to stay safe from the dangers that lurked outside on the streets. It was where they went when they ran away from home, and it was where they found peace.

Time had passed, however. With Mayisha's retirement party quickly approaching and the future of the ranch in jeopardy, their safety, and their way of life, was all up for grabs.

ANTHONY NOTICED FURY'S limp when he first arrived at the ranch that morning. The eldest of the cowboys, he also had the sharpest eyes on the ranch. During the week, Anthony's workday began at 5 a.m. and lasted well into the early afternoon. It was his job to keep up with all twelve of the horses, feed and care for them. It had been almost six months since Fury's phantom limp developed, which Anthony at first suspected was clubfoot, a condition that involved asymmetrical hooves.

Now Anthony believed the limp had more to do with the way Fury's shoe had been fitted. Everyone knew the farrier liked to cut corners when nobody was there to supervise him, and more so, everyone knew it had to do with race: ranches run by white families probably got better service from their horseshoe person. Every time Fury applied pressure to the foot he got agitated. If more resources had been available on the ranch, like in the old days, then Fury would have seen a specialist. But with limited funds, all Anthony could do was apply more medicated balm to dull the pain.

Back in front of the ranch, on Caldwell Street, there was still no sign of the other cowboys. Only the sounds of Mexican *banda* music played off in the distance, while commercial planes and helicopters flew in and out of Compton's local airport.

After the trio finished grooming their horses, they each left to go run errands. Anthony had to drop off his granddaughter at her aunt's home, Charles drove to the Jordan Downs Housing projects to see his family, and Keenan had to head back home to pick up some riding gear. Kenneth, whose home bordered the ranch's back wall, was supposed to have already been out of his early alcohol counseling class by then, but he was nowhere to be found.

Getting each of the ten cowboys to ride together was one of the biggest challenges for the group these days. The cowboy life-styles they were living—big street rides, ranch work, and rodeo competitions—were sometimes at odds with the realities of day-to-day life. Only Tre and Charles continued to train and compete in their respective events, bareback riding and show jumping. Keiara was still rehabbing her back after an injury that continued to keep her out of barrel racing. The rest of the gang wrestled with the challenges of putting food on the table for themselves and their families, and with growing families and more mouths to feed, sacrifices had to be made.

In the meantime, Randy Hook drove his dark blue Chevy Malibu south on Wilmington Avenue in the direction of the ranch. His jet-black tinted car windows rattled with the sounds of bass-heavy rap music. Since he had taken over as the Compton Cowboys' leader and begun to take more responsibility for the ranch in anticipation of Mayisha's upcoming retirement, the level of anxiety and stress that he experienced had drastically increased. The only way to remedy the pressure was to isolate himself, riding his horse late at night around the farms and taking long drives through the city. Driving alone allowed him to sit with his thoughts and put him out of the reach of those who often relied on him for answers that he didn't always have. He could momentarily escape the pressures of being a father, a brother, and the leader of the last black cowboys in Compton.

As he waited for the light to turn green at the intersection of Alondra and Wilmington, a group of five black teenagers gathered at the cross light. They were no older than fifteen years and showed signs of the life he and his friends had once lived. They wore red shoes and jackets and held bags of Flamin' Hot Cheetos and sodas in their hands the same way he used to. They reminded him of the Akrite party crew that he and some of the cowboys had created as teenagers as a way to stay together after they left the Compton Junior Posse. The crew threw weekend parties and were known around Compton as one of the best party organizers. Like the Akrites, the group of teenagers stood in unison, creating a 360-degree circle of vision around them for protection. They hung on to each other because they were all each other had. Randy thought about his party crew days and he and Carlton's eighteen-year-old celebration party that had left two of their friends dead, forcing them to disband and abandon the scene altogether.

In a matter of moments, Randy's nostalgia immediately wore off as some of the teens turned to face in his direction. In seconds they transformed from friendly nostalgic reminders to potential threats. They saw only a possible foe in a dark blue car with tinted windows, not someone who had once stood on the same corner as them with the same intentions—someone with the same wild spirit. Though Randy was still on neutral territory, he kept a sharp eye on the group. The farms belonged to the Farm Dog Crips, which included his friends and family, while the area west of Wilmington Avenue belonged to their enemies, the Nutty Blocc Crips gang. The group continued to stare at his car, anticipating action.

When the light turned green, Randy quickly tapped the ignition pedal and sped away, past the 7-Eleven and the Louisiana Fried Chicken, and within seconds the group became small figures in his rearview mirror, fading out like the memories of his youth.

IT HAD BEEN only a few weeks since Randy started living out of the trunk of his car. His backseat was full of clothes, shoes, and anything else he could find room for. His most prized cowboy hats were gently stacked on top of boxes, leaving only a slight space in between two large boxes to see out of his rearview mirror.

The apartment that he and Mariah, his high school sweetheart and girlfriend, had been renting in the San Fernando Valley had gotten too expensive, and with Luxe, their newborn baby, finding the means to afford the rent was a financial strain for them. So the young family moved back to the farms, back into the community where they had first met more than fifteen years earlier, back to the community they had once left to find peace of mind.

On top of that, Randy had quit his job and now hoped to generate an income directing the ranch and its organization when his aunt Mayisha officially retired.

He had big dreams. Living out of his car, however, wasn't what the twenty-eight-year-old with a college and graduate degree had imagined he would be doing, but it was the only choice he had. His father's house was full, and the middle home on the ranch was better suited for his baby boy and Mariah. Nights alone were at times the only cure for the insomnia that he had experienced since he was a child.

He made a left at the intersection of Caldwell and Wilmington, at the gas station where so many of his friends had been shot and killed, and a minute later pulled into the driveway. The sound system in the back of his trunk continued to rattle the tinted car windows.

"Where the fuck is everyone?" he said to himself as he slammed his car door and walked toward the back of the ranch, carrying a box of black Compton Cowboys T-shirts. "I told everyone to be ready to go by ten a.m. This some bullshit!"

Randy's frustration with the group had been growing in recent months. Since he had assumed command of the Compton Cowboys and the ranch's day-to-day operations, some were beginning to feel like he wasn't suited to lead the group. The bickering and talking behind his back were taking a toll on his emotional health. Sleepless nights quickly turned into moody mornings. Sometimes, when he was alone and out of sight of the group, the stress would overcome him and he'd burst into uncontrollable sobs. The crying temporarily relieved him of the pain, but it only magnified the loneliness.

Randy had fought hard to be able to get the cowboys to ride in this year's parade. He had worked to reestablish the group as active members in the community by attending city council meetings, advocating for the rights of horse riders in Compton. As Mayisha leaned closer into retirement, the ranch's youth program slowly began to dwindle, leaving local youth with limited afterschool and weekend options. On top of this, assuming the responsibilities of managing the ranch would be challenging. Mayisha's commitment was matched only by her decades of advocating for the Compton Junior Posse, the organization she started in 1988 as a way to provide Compton's youth with an alternative to gangs and violence. Filling her shoes seemed like a daunting task, but, like her, Randy was inspired to break age-old stereotypes about black cowboys and create opportunities for young children who were faced with the pressures of joining street gangs like he once was.

Randy wanted to create a new image for black riders in Compton that aligned with the life experiences that he and other members of the Compton Cowboys had lived. He wanted to make cowboy culture accessible and, most of all, cool. Riding in the parade would be a way to introduce the Compton Cowboys to the city for the first time since they rode in the parade over fifteen years earlier. Whether or not the other guys knew it, this was a day that Randy had been thinking about for months—he knew how important it was to the future of the group and his aunt's legacy.

They were not the only black horse riders in Los Angeles; there was another group based at a nearby South Central ranch known as "the Hill." Its stables had recently burned down, and most believed the cause was arson. The Hill, like the farms, was a place where newly arrived black cowboys from the South could go to ride. They were different from the Compton Cowboys, though; they came from different neighborhoods and were separated by miles and gang affiliations. The Hill was located in a Blood neighborhood, while the farms were in an area controlled by the Crips.

"Carlton, go get your fucking horse ready," Randy said as he made his way back inside the house. "I swear, you always on that bullshit." He continued to yell at his brother while slamming the back door loud enough for Byron to hear in the front of the house. "Always, always," he repeated.

"I done already took care of my horse," Carlton shouted. "We was out there early this morning! Don't be coming out here yelling at me like that, cuz!"

Byron stepped out of the back door and ignored the commotion.

"Aye, you got fifty cents?" he asked Randy.

"Not right now, man," Randy replied and continued walking. "Not right now, Byron."

Only seconds separated Randy and Carlton in birth order, but the two couldn't have been more different. Randy was loud, gregarious, and felt comfortable in leadership roles. The sides of his head were closely trimmed, leaving only a small Afro-textured bit of hair on the top. Carlton preferred a calmer, quieter approach and often stood in the background. He wore his hair in dreadlocks. Whenever Carlton had a problem, Randy was there to help solve it through their daily bickering. One day it would be about finances, another it could stem from an issue with being punctual, or not asking permission to wear the other's hat. The quarrels never ended.

Keenan was dropped off in front of the ranch in a blue Toyota Camry at 10:40 a.m.—forty minutes after he was supposed to have been there. He was wearing a black cowboy hat and carrying a blue duffel bag that he carried close to his body. He had forgotten some of his clothes at home and had hurried back to get them.

"Damn, you really are a cowboy," the Uber driver said as he

waited for Keenan to get out of the car while looking at the horses in the stalls at the back of the ranch. "You wasn't lying."

Keenan smiled and shut the car door behind him.

Charles arrived ten minutes later wearing a black-and-white baseball-style Compton Cowboys T-shirt, tight-fitting black jeans, and a new pair of Nike Air Jordans.

"How the fuck you get yours already?" Keenan asked as Charles approached him in the back of the ranch.

"Oh, this little thing?" He brandished a full-toothed grin and chuckled, pointing down at his T-shirt. "Man, you know I got the plug. I stay lookin' fly."

Randy sat down and texted everyone in the group chat. "WHERE YALL AT?" he wrote. "Y'all were supposed to have been here at 10 a.m."

At the current rate, four out of ten cowboys wouldn't be enough to fill a riding line. It worried Randy. He feared that he and his friends would be the laughingstock of the parade, a far cry from the spectacular forty-person marches the Compton Junior Posse used to put on every year.

This was the part of the job that he hated the most. Since their days as members of the Akrites, the cowboys had always looked up to Randy for his leadership. When he went away for school, at Occidental College, he still continued to lead. Even when he was a graduate student at Cal State University, Northridge, his friends had relied on him for support. But sometimes being a member of the cowboys and their manager was difficult. It meant he had to be everyone's friend and their leader, which required making tough decisions from time to time. Half the battle was getting people to show up to rides and events on time. The other half was managing the multiple personalities in the group that sometimes clashed.

"We're always just one fight away from destroying all that we've built," he often said. "This shit could all come crashing down."

The group's cohesiveness had been put to the test earlier in the year, during the summer, when a physical altercation broke out between Tre, one of the youngest cowboys, and Charles. Someone in the group had posted a photo of children riding horses on the ranch on the group's Instagram page and written a caption about the importance of being good role models for Compton's youth. Hundreds of people liked the image and showed their support by commenting on the photo. Some of their followers shared their own story about the impact of black cowboys in the city of Compton.

The post, however, prompted Tre's baby's mother to unleash a series of public comments about Tre's parenting. She claimed that he was a deadbeat father and unwilling to help provide for his son and pointed out the hypocrisy of the Instagram post. Within minutes different members of the group wrote to Tre in the cowboys' group chat asking him about the situation. Charles joked about Tre's situation, claiming that Tre didn't know how to "control" the mother of his child.

The conversation quickly escalated when both started to call each other "bitches" as the rest of the cowboys read on in the group chat. "Bitch, bitch, bitch, bitch, bitch," Charles emphatically wrote. While Tre had ongoing issues with his child's mother, Charles was deeply enveloped in his own child custody battle. The argument escalated to a series of physical threats. "We gonna see who's a bitch the next time I see you," Tre said to him.

The cowboys' group chat remained silent for the next few days. Everyone felt the tension, but nobody dared to step in between the two. Anthony had seen situations like these turn dangerous before and called both Tre and Charles to arrange a meeting.

"Put on some boxing gloves," Anthony said to each of them individually. "Settle whatever issue you have with one another that way."

Both men shut his idea down. They didn't want to settle anything just yet—being called a bitch was one of the highest forms of insult on the farms. But a few days later, Tre learned that Charles was at the ranch with his younger brother Rambo. When he arrived half an hour later, a fight immediately ensued.

Tre had a physical advantage over Charles. He was six feet tall and still had the same muscular arms and broad shoulders that he had developed while playing football in high school and college and competing in the rodeo circuit. The ferocity of his punches was the culmination of years of pain and anger trapped deep inside him. Charles's brother Rambo, who was among those standing in a circle around them, had seen enough. When one of Tre's right hooks landed against his jaw and sent his older brother flying to the ground, Rambo ran behind Tre and tackled him. Charles recovered consciousness moments later and began kicking the side of Tre's body while his brother did the same. What began as a one-on-one fight between Charles and Tre transformed into a three-person melee.

When it ended, Tre hobbled away from the ranch with a broken leg and blood spit coming out of his mouth. Charles and Rambo tasted the same blood in their own mouths and had their own bruises on their faces.

Under normal circumstances, fights weren't considered out of the norm between the cowboys. When words didn't relay the appropriate message, fists were used as a form of communication. Different punches, like words, had different meanings, tones, and intonation. Each punch came with its own lexicon. However, this time was different. The Harris brothers had broken one of the unwritten rules in the 'hood that day: they had both jumped Tre and would have to live with the consequences.

For Tre, however, it was more than just about his honor, it was also about his livelihood: his broken leg would keep him from competing in the rodeo circuit for months.

ANTHONY ARRIVED BACK at the ranch an hour later in a brown 1991 Ford truck that he had bought months earlier from one of his Mexican neighbors in the Imperial Courts housing projects. He called it his *paisa* truck—as Mexican men who wore traditional Mexican cowboy clothing were called in Compton, especially those who drove pickup trucks with gardening or construction equipment in their truck beds. Anthony preferred the comfort of his paisa truck over anything else. It was unassuming and helped him keep a low profile on the streets. With large rust stains on its exterior and sporting a large crack that spanned the entire front windshield, the truck was a far cry from the flashy cars he used to ride in in his twenties, but at this point in his life it provided him with exactly what he needed, and allowed him to drive safely to and from the ranch every day.

Like the horses that he rode, the truck offered him protection from the police or local gangs. The police would just drive on past, not bothering to consider the ragtag truck or the person inside it as a threat.

The parade was set to start in an hour and there was still no sign of the rest of the group. Xavier, an alumnus of the Junior Posse and a friend of the cowboys, had shown up to ride with the cowboys at Randy's request. There were now six, still not the entire group but more than before. After deliberating inside his head, Randy decided it was time to ride out.

"The rest of the guys are going to have to meet us over there," he shouted to everyone as they continued to brush their horses and clean out horseshoes with metal hooks. "If we don't leave soon, we're going to be late," he said.

It was a big day for the cowboys. It was the first time in over fifteen years that the city of Compton would see them officially ride. When they rode as children, eager parade attendees lined up on both sides of the streets to see them ride on Compton Boulevard. Those who weren't old enough to ride proudly carried the blue Compton Junior Posse flag in front of the group.

Both the cowboys and the city had almost completely transformed since then. The blue Junior Posse color scheme was now replaced by black-and-white Old English–style writing with more flair and swagger. The shirts on their backs read COMPTON COWBOYS.

For the new generation of riders, looking good was a big part of the cowboy lifestyle that they hoped to create. Mayisha's dream of sharply dressed cowboys didn't always align with the vision they had for themselves. Some of them thought they were being forced to dress like squares. Now they had the option of putting on traditional cowboy garb and enjoyed the freedom of riding in Nike Air Jordans, Gucci belts, and other designer clothes. Both their clothes and their horses became the armor that protected them.

Everyone's armor looked different in Compton. The Campanella Park Pirus, a westside Compton Blood gang, wore red bandanas draped softly on the side of their shoulders and yelled out phrases like "suwuu" at any given moment. The red armor they wore both stopped and attracted bullets. The Acacia Blocc Crips from the eastside yelled out words like "owiee, owiee" as a rallying call to both friends and foes. The color of their armor was dark blue.

Most people in the city of Compton, however, weren't affiliated with gangs. Their color was that which they had been born into, the delicate black and brown skin that stood between them and the world. This, too, was armor.

Keenan and his horse Sonny were the first pair to make their way out of the ranch's gates and onto Caldwell. Wearing a crisp black cowboy hat, dark sunglasses, tight-fitting black jeans, and black boots, Keenan looked as ready to step onto a western movie set as he did to ride in a family Christmas parade. The white T-shirt that he wore that morning was replaced by a large black CC shirt that clung close to his body. His freshly braided hair was pulled back into two large braids that tightly gripped his scalp and were tied together by two small purple rubber bands. Only small traces of the dry white flakes of his eczema skin condition showed on his scalp. Except for his hands, every part of his body was covered by black clothes, revealing only multiple tattoos on each of the hands and fingers that held on to Sonny's reins.

Caldwell's street residents stood outside their homes as the cowboys made their way out to the street. One by one—like they had done for years—they trotted past the safety of the black gates that separated them from the outside world.

"I'm so happy y'all are back," one woman said to Carlton as she stood on the street with bright green rollers in her hair. "It brings me so much joy to see y'all again." A group of neighbors snapped photos and videos with their cell phones. One boy approached the cowboys and took a selfie video. "I'm with the Compton Cowboys, y'all!" he yelled into his phone several times before finally walking away.

As more and more people gathered on the street to take photos with the cowboys, Sonny began to feel anxious and almost jerked Keenan off his back. Fifteen years earlier, a plastic water gun had gone off near his head, and the fear of that day had stayed with him. Every time he heard a sharp sound, he'd panic. Fortunately, Keenan understood Sonny's trauma—he had lived through some of it himself. Loud, sharp sounds also made him feel anxious; they reminded him of the gunshots he and his friends had fled from on numerous occasions and those that took his horse's life when he was in high school.

"Whoooa, Sonny," he whispered into his ear as an unknown car drove past the ranch playing loud rap music. "It's okay, you're safe with me."

Charles was the last cowboy to ride out of the ranch. Unlike everyone else, he refused to wear a cowboy hat and boots, choosing instead a new pair of Air Jordans and a black New York Yankees baseball hat. It was a far cry from the traditional dress he was forced to wear as an English-style jumper: britches, riding helmet, and long black show boots. When Mayisha switched the program's style of riding from western to English years ago, Charles was the only member of the group who had fully embraced it.

As they all waited in front of Louie's house, the adoring fans who had gathered to take their picture made their way inside their homes to prepare for their own participation in the parade. Louie stepped out on the porch and looked at the group of children he had helped raise. As Randy and Carlton's single father, being a parent extended beyond raising his own two children. Every member of the Compton Cowboys had spent days and nights in his home as children. They had shared countless meals and gone on vacations and camping trips together. Being black cowboys was as much about having a community where you could be your unapologetic self as it was about riding, and Louis helped provide that.

Louie wore his Occidental College T-shirt that morning with pride, proud of Randy, his only son to have graduated from college. The sight of the cowboys in front of his home stirred up emotions that he hadn't felt in years. He saw boys whom he had spent countless hours driving to and from rodeo circuit competitions. Some of them now had their own families to look after, but though they were much older and had more facial hair, they would always be the same boys he remembered. He grabbed his phone from his pocket and took a photo to preserve the memory. The last time they rode together in the parade as teenagers, part of him believed that the legacy of black cowboys would end on the farms. But seeing them together again brought him to tears. He was filled with emotion, hopeful of the future in spite of the impending changes that the ranch was experiencing.

"Let's ride," Randy said, fixing the brim of his black Stetson hat and looking at his phone. "Yaaaa! . . . Yaaaa!" he yelled at his horse.

Randy, Carlton, Anthony, Keenan, Charles, and Xavier trotted down the street on their horses. The sound of the horses' hooves blended in with the other sounds on the farms, coming together in a synchronized, orchestral fashion, a series of rhythms that ended in a dramatic crescendo—a 'hood symphony of sorts. The other Cowboys—Terrance, Layton, Tre, and Keiara, had to work and weren't able to take the day off. Kenneth would be joining them later. The sounds of their horses on the street reminded them of their days as members of the Junior Posse. Mayisha used to lead the way, wearing a long dark blue or orange African kente dress while she rode her horse. The posse would trail behind her, listening to her every command. "Paraaaaaaade, march," she would yell to get the group going.

As they approached the intersection of Tichenor and Oleander, Keenan was reminded of his horse Flower, who had been the victim of a hit-and-run accident when he was a teenager. Every block elicited a different memory for each rider. Some were joyous, some weren't. These were the same streets they had grown up riding in, and riding together reminded them of the days when their entire lives revolved around horses. Things seemed so much simpler then for everyone in the group.

Several groups of Latino families were making their way out of their homes as the cowboys approached the storm canals, an area that many of the cowboys had used as a hideout spot when enemy gangs wandered through the area during their youth.

One family was in the process of boarding a Toyota family van, while another sat in their garden on lawn chairs. One of the children, a boy no older than seven years old, stormed out of the house wearing nothing but a pair of polka-dotted swim trunks and goggles on his head, inciting immediate laughs from each of the cowboys as they rode past the scene. It took his mother minutes to catch and discipline him.

"I told you to not run out of the house that way," she yelled in Spanish as she stood in front of him and pointed at his face. "Get in the car!"

He ran into the family van full of beach equipment where his father waited impatiently in the front seat, scrolling on his cell phone while speaking to the child's older brother in the back.

Next door, a group of twelve middle-aged Mexican men stood on horses wearing matching brown leather vests that read "Los Rancheros de Compton." They gathered outside the home of one of their members, mounted on well-trained Friesian horses that danced on command to the sound of someone's cell phone playing northern Mexican banda music, blaring brass instruments with thumping drums.

Los Rancheros were a Mexican riding group from the farms who had been in the area for years. They had ridden with the cowboys in past parades and had established an amicable relationship with them. When the Mexicans arrived in the early 1980s, they were a minority; the farms were comprised of entirely black cowboys and riders. The rancheros were part of waves of Mexican immigrants who left farm life in Mexican states like Jalisco and Michoacán for the promise of providing more for their families than life in Mexico could. They pooled their money by living in multifamily homes and bought property, creating semblances of the lives they had left behind. Many of the Mexican families that migrated to the farms settled in contentious blocks and experienced the crime and violence of the crack cocaine era of the 1980s and early 1990s.

This was also an era when many black families—some of them middle class—were forced out of the farms because of increasing rents and the continued threat of violence. Some of them took their horses with them, choosing to resettle in cities around Los Angeles like San Bernardino, Fontana, and Moreno Valley, where they established new black horse-riding communities. Since then Compton's Latino population had increased to almost 70 percent of the entire city.

"Hola, amigos!" Keenan yelled out to the group of riders. "Qué onda? What's up?" he asked as they greeted one another.

"Buenos días, Keenan," one of them replied.

Los Rancheros were accompanied by a six-year-old boy who

rode alongside them on a white pony, tagging along closely behind his father. "Espérame, Papá!" he yelled to his father as the group began to leave him.

Racial tensions between Latinos and African-Americans were common in the city of Compton. But on the farms, horses had brought both groups together in ways that were unimaginable outside of them. When finding common ground between African-Americans and Latinos proved challenging for local politicians, particularly during the height of the Fruit Town Piru and Tortilla Flats gang war, the act of riding horses together helped people reach a truce. The Compton parade was one of the few times when the entire city would unite. On the streets, the Crip and Blood gangs declared truces during the parade to allow people to safely attend the festivities. The truces ensured that local marching bands from high schools like Compton High and Compton Centennial could compete for bragging rights.

Back in the Compton Junior Posse days, the parade also required hours of committed and often strenuous practice that took place in front of the ranch on Caldwell. Mayisha had always circled the date on the calendar—the parade was an opportunity to show the city the effort her riders were putting into a noble cause, horse riding. Practice usually began about a month before the parade and lasted two to three hours after school every day. Sometimes they would practice on horseback, but most of the time they were relegated to rehearsing without horses on the street. "Remember to keep your back straight, smile, and wave with one hand and keep your other hand on the reins," the cowboys remembered Mayisha telling them when they were children. "We're setting an example to the whole city, so be at your best, you hear?" Moments before the parade would start, she'd turn to her riders and remind them, "Don't be acting a fool."

The group had gotten significantly smaller since their youth, and fear of the future crept into their minds as they continued to ride toward the parade's starting point on Compton Boulevard. As children, many of them had enjoyed riding in the parade, but as teenagers they'd stopped. Cowboys weren't cool, according to Randy and Carlton, but because they were Mayisha's nephews and next-door neighbors, they were forced to ride anyway when they were in high school. The other cowboys believed that riding horses wouldn't help their dating lives because the girls they knew were only interested in dating athletes or gangsters.

This year felt a bit different for the cowboys. They had a lot to prove and it was their first time riding under the CC moniker. It would be their chance to show friends and family that they could succeed without the elders who had taught them how to ride when they were children. More importantly, they wanted to prove to Mayisha that they could do it on their own.

THE 'WOOD CONTINUED to be passed back and forth between the cowboys as they rode past Compton High School's light blue walls. Anthony began recording the ride on his cell phone and shouting out to friends of his as he rode past them.

"What up, my nigga!" he yelled to a car full of friends. "You see us!"

A silver early 2000s BMW sedan, with unmarked license plates, pulled up to the group from its rear. The sound of its loud rap music caused everyone—including the horses—to immediately turn around.

It was Rambo, Charles's younger brother.

"What up, cuz!" he yelled as his slender body stuck out of the window. He playfully threw up the Grape Street Crips gang sign to Charles amid the sounds of Young Dolph playing loudly from the inside of his car. "Y'all ready for the parade?"

"Hell yeah, my nigga," Charles said, while others from the group greeted Rambo and also nodded in agreement.

"We ready," Anthony said, overenunciating the ending of the word.

Rambo had also grown up with the group as a member of the Junior Posse but had chosen gang-banging over horses as a teenager. Unlike his brother, Rambo ended up choosing the streets and was jumped into the Grape Street Crips. He was frequently in and out of prison and still associated with the group even though he hadn't ridden in more than fifteen years.

Rambo drove along the left side of the group and turned up his music, providing a lively soundtrack while simultaneously live-streaming the ride on his phone.

"You see us!" he yelled at the top of his lungs for his social media followers. "We the motherfucking Compton Cowboys!"

The group was slowly increasing in size. Minutes after Rambo started to trail them, another rider named Eugene, a twelve-year-old who lived in the Nutty Blocc neighborhood, run by the hostile Crips gang, caught up to the group. He was riding a short-haired brown pony. He was one of the few youth riders in the farms and looked to each of the cowboys as role models.

"Put this on," Randy said as he tossed Eugene a CC shirt.

"Thanks, man," Eugene said with a big grin on his face.

Riding through the streets of Compton brought back a series of different memories for the group. Anthony rode past the gas station on Alondra and Acacia with a heavy heart. His best friend, Black, had been shot and killed there years before. Black was the person who introduced Anthony to Mayisha and first encouraged him to ride horses as a child.

They rode past the Compton Courthouse where many of them had been charged with crimes as minors and adults. They rode past the mural of a jubilant and toothy-grinned newly elected president Barack Obama on the side of the courthouse, an image that at this point felt more satirical than an actual representation of Compton. The hope Obama had promised never quite found its way to the Hub City between 2008 and 2016; high murder and unemployment rates never changed.

Kenneth finally appeared on Ebony, a black Tennessee Walker, moments before the parade began. His dreads hung below his black Stetson hat, and his Compton Cowboys T-shirt squeezed his torso. He had spent the entire morning at his court-ordered alcohol counseling class after being charged with his second DUI early in 2018.

As the group was slowly ushered in line toward the starting point, each cowboy seemed to be locked in a deep state of reminiscence.

Anthony thought about the time he had spent incarcerated and had flashes of the horse paintings that had given him something to look forward to. Keenan thought about Flower and the many parades they rode together in before she was killed. Randy thought about the dreams his father had about black cowboys and how he had always wanted his sons to have positive images of them in ways that he never had growing up. Charles thought about the example he could set for his children and hoped they never had to grow up in the same conditions that he did. Horses, he believed, could save their lives.

The group turned their reins to the left and began trotting on

Compton Boulevard as soon as the parade conductor signaled them to move.

"Stay close to each other, y'all," Randy shouted. "Two per line, two per line."

Randy found himself echoing the same words that Mayisha had once shouted to them as teenagers. Her influence was never too far away. "Bring up the line!" he yelled.

Crowds stood on both sides of the empty boulevard to watch them ride. They rode with elegance and assertiveness, carrying on the tradition of the legacy of Compton's black cowboys that had been around since the 1950s. They rode past Burris Avenue, Sloan, Poinsettia, and Long Beach Boulevard waving at people on both sides of the streets. It was the first time many of the horses had been in the parade, and the sounds of the streets, people, and music made some of them feel uneasy. Anthony carefully tugged on Koda's reins and slowly withdrew from the group as people on both sides of the street continued to wave at the cowboys. Anthony waved and smiled back.

The black families that had filled the streets during his youth were now almost entirely replaced by brown faces. The stores and fast-food restaurants had remained, but black families that had made the Christmas parade a staple in their lives had been replaced by faces he didn't recognize. The Compton he had once known had changed dramatically since his days with the Junior Posse.

What stayed the same, however, were the shields that each person carried with them. Members of the South Side Crips leaned on the side of an abandoned building.

The cowboys approached the main stage, where an announcer held a microphone connected to a loudspeaker, acknowledging the groups that had participated in the day's events.

"Everyone ride in a straight line!" Randy yelled to everyone as they neared the stage. "Let's show them what we got."

And the group lined up just so.

The crowd's cheers intensified as the cowboys neared the center stage. Every cowboy felt something different, but they each knew that riding together was the one thing that had preserved their friendship throughout the years. Through the quarreling and confusion and deaths of friends and family, they continued to ride. It was the glue that kept them together. They were the glue that kept their community together.

Eugene looked around in astonishment as he continued to ride in his first-ever parade. Keenan stared long and hard at him and thought about the innocence he saw on Eugene's face, remembering his own innocence and the first time he rode in the parade.

At twelve, Eugene was too young to understand what life had taught Keenan as a twenty-seven-year-old black man in the city of Compton: that the world would never fully accept the sight of black people on horses—that the world would do everything in its power to keep him off his horse. Keenan wanted Eugene to understand the privilege of entering a lineage of black cowboys in Compton that had existed long before he was born; neighborhood elders like Mr. Colbert, Van, Myron, and Marcus, who were part of individual groups of African-Americans who saw the farms as an idyllic location for their horses and their families.

Keenan wanted to tell Eugene that he hoped he never strayed too far away from his horse. He wanted to grab him by the shoulders, look him in the eyes, and tell him that his horse could protect him. That his horse could, if he wanted, become a defense mechanism in a city that would do everything in its power to injure him.

Keenan wanted to tell him these things, but he knew that Eugene, like he once did, years ago, would have to learn on his own.

The announcer took the podium and began to read: "Ladies and gentlemen, straight out of the Richland Farms, the Compton Cowboys are alumni of the nonprofit youth organization the Compton Junior Posse, who use horses to keep kids off the streets."

The cowboys trotted past the stage, waving proudly at their city. They received the loudest applause of the day. The brown faces in the audience cheered because they had never seen black cowboys before. The black faces cheered because it had been years since they had. The cheers forced smiles from the edges of each cowboy's mouth as they continued riding west on Compton Boulevard, toward the farms, toward the fading sun.

THROUGH HER EYES

MAYISHA BACKED HER WHITE CHEVROLET Silverado pickup truck out of the farm's driveway the same way she had done thousands of times over the past thirty years of her life. She looked behind her right shoulder, put her arm on the passenger seat, and pushed the gas pedal slowly. After nearly missing Anthony's truck by inches on her way out, she switched gears, putting her truck into drive while listening to an R&B station.

With light chestnut skin and a full build, Mayisha wore a long multicolored dress. The metal band on her left wrist shone brightly in the sun, while her left arm hung freely on the outside of her truck door as she made her way west on Caldwell toward the hardware store. She passed a series of trucks parked on both sides of streets only made for vehicles and horses. Heavy-duty trucks like hers were a staple on the farms—they made transporting large machinery and pulling horse trailers easy.

Mayisha had tried different hairstyles over the years, but at this point in her life her hair was in thin, tightly coiled dreads that stretched down to her shoulders and were easy to manage. The reflection of her face on the driver's-side window was that of someone who, after so many years of evading the aging process, was finally confronted by it. Her hair was almost fully grey, a silver undertone replacing the black hair that she had been known for through the years. She paused to look at her own reflection in the mirror one last time before focusing her eyes on the road ahead of her.

It was only a few days before her retirement party and there was still a lot of work to do on the ranch. A group of her closest friends were organizing the event, but Mayisha could not bear the thought of not being able to help out with her own party, so she did what she had always done best—she worked. After all, the party was going to be on her ranch, and as long as she was still a part of the organization, she would ensure that it ran as smoothly as possible. This was the same spirit that made her one of the most successful black female real estate agents in Los Angeles during the 1990s. It was the same spirit that helped create one of the first black-owned horse ranches in the United States.

EARLIER IN THE year, after much speculation and a series of health problems, Mayisha had decided it was time to hand over the reins of the ranch to her nephew, Randy.

Taking control of the ranch had always been a priority for Randy. As one of the few college-educated members of the cowboys, he understood that maintaining it required more than just the ability to teach youth how to ride horses. Mayisha had excelled at leading the ranch, which also required becoming a leader in the community. The ranch in many ways sustained the spirit of the community. As the ranch went, so did the community.

The ranch was more than just horses for the cowboys. Losing it would mean losing a part of Compton's ecosystem. It was a place to train and ride horses, sure, but more importantly, it was a place where people could *belong*. The ranch was home to a series of interweaving relationships that they each called home. It functioned as a renewable source of life, where trauma could be reconciled with the joy of riding horses. It was where friendships were preserved. It was the memory center of their culture, where

Anthony and Keenan first learned about the legacy of black cowboys. And now, if things went as they hoped, they were in a position to pass on that tradition, that sanctuary, to the next generation.

Over the years the ranch had been kept alive through different income streams. Its board members, many of whom were wealthy white businesspeople, kept it going with their generous donations, public and private grants, and scholarships through a network of like-minded benevolent sponsors. Mayisha excelled at promoting her organization to rich celebrities in Los Angeles like Magic Johnson and a host of others who had supported her over the years. Her vision for the ranch was directly linked to the vision for her community. Getting kids on horses, she believed, dramatically lowered the chances of gang involvement. Her model worked. It helped young people perform better in school by incentivizing them with rides and trips in and around Los Angeles. Horses also had a way of helping young people heal from different forms of trauma; equine therapy became an informal tool to help children become softer, more compassionate members of the community.

When the cowboys officially rebanded in 2016, it was after years of being apart. Life had gotten in the way of the bonds that they had formed as children. Many of them had stopped coming to the ranch. Randy had moved out to the San Fernando Valley where he was attending graduate school and living with Mariah, the mother of his child. Layton had been living in the neighborhood but only occasionally came around to the ranch whenever Randy was back in town. Tre had been competing professionally on the rodeo circuit throughout the United States, excelling as one of the nation's best bareback riders. Keenan was working as a sous-chef at a restaurant near downtown Los Angeles, Charles was show jumping, and Kenneth was going on occasional rides through the neighborhood. Keiara, still battling with the loss of her brother and horse, had taken a break from riding.

Forming the Compton Cowboys became a way to not just ride together again, but also to give back to the community that had raised them.

Some of the cowboys recognized that it wouldn't be an easy transition. Keenan worried the most. He understood that taking over the ranch would require a crash course on finances, outreach, and civic participation. It was an exchange of power that resembled postcolonial governments, only this time it was the ruler's nephew who was taking over. The cowboys would have to find an entirely new board, since the older board members were also retiring.

In other words, taking over the ranch would require either finding a group of wealthy people to help fund the operation or creating other revenue streams. At the beginning of the year when Keenan was asked to become one of the board members, he was unemployed and had just been fired from working as a chef at a restaurant in Los Angeles. He was cooking part-time and making dishes at home that he could sell to friends and family. Saying yes was a big undertaking and the job was growing by the day. For the cowboys and Keenan especially, it felt like a make-or-break situation. The biggest hurdle was themselves, what Keenan called a "crabs in a bucket mentality," meaning a type of struggle for survival that forced people to compete in situations where working together would produce a more favorable outcome. In Compton, it was both love and hate that drew people together. You were bound by blood, but blood didn't always guarantee love. The cowboys had been raised in a place where people automatically saw spaces as contested territory, and each other, too often, as adversaries.

Now, in 2018, two years after the official banding, there had been issues that had only exacerbated some of Keenan's worries. The brotherhood that they shared since they were children was durable. It was built on a sense of trust only described through those who would die for you. But in recent years, adulthood had gotten in the way. Tre and Charles's fight had strained the bond that they shared, and their stress and worry sometimes turned into shouting matches that threatened to turn physical.

During the transition, when a few of the cowboys would get hired for commercial advertisements, questions about money and exposure arose in ways that were never an issue in Mayisha's day. Kenneth became one of the most sought-after cowboys for shoots, and he bragged about it on social media. The year had brought the cowboys more notoriety for their commercial appeal—the sight of black cowboys was as jarring as it was enticing for brands—but it also brought increased visibility to the ranch. New people were hanging out at the ranch, bringing the streets into what had been neutral territory.

Rashid, Mayisha's oldest son, a lifelong member of the Farm Dog Crips, and one of the first to ride on the farms, had moved into Mayisha's home when she moved to Norco, a community located fifty miles or so east of L.A. As someone with a deep connection to the ranch's history, he often took on the responsibility of protecting the ranch despite pleas not to from Randy and his father. Rashid had worked as the ranch hand before Anthony was released, but in recent years he had dedicated his life to becoming a traveling electrician. The cowboys respected him. After all, he was one of the 'hood's last original gangsters and he was family.

But Rashid's presence on the ranch also slowed down their plans. It was hard for him to see the cowboys as adults. In his eyes they were still the same children whom he helped raise. Getting him to let go and see them as responsible adults was one of the cowboys' biggest concerns.

As the cowboys continued to plan for the transition, Mayisha continued to have worries about the image that the cowboys presented. At the same time, her own actions sometimes negatively impacted the cowboys' hopes to keep the future of the ranch alive.

If anyone understood Mayisha, it was Randy. He knew how much the ranch meant to her, and how difficult it must be for her to know that its fate was not entirely secure. She'd been at the helm for so many years and created everything. Randy recognized that she had the power to knock it all down herself if she wanted to. Getting Mayisha to cede control was one of the toughest challenges he faced. The ranch was like her child, now thirty years old, and who wants to see their child find a new parent?

But the ranch meant everything to Randy, and he felt ready to run it. He had spent nearly his entire life watching other people run the organization, some of whom didn't have the same connection as him. A year before the ranch was to be handed over to Randy, a Latino man was hired to run it. After a year, the man left amid disagreements over the vision for the ranch. The event left Randy with a bad taste in his mouth. The guy never had a chance, he felt, and it had to do with rootedness. How does an outsider come in and deal with Compton? How does someone who's never set foot on Compton turf expect to transition young hoodlums into thriving citizens? Randy understood that you had to be from the 'hood, grow up in the 'hood, to make that change. And who was better suited for that than himself?

As Mayisha's retirement approached, Randy began to learn about the financial realities. In a few months, without new funding, the ranch would have to close. His aunt's retirement also meant that the board and its funding streams would end as well. The reality crept closer as each day passed. If Mayisha left and Randy couldn't keep a community of supporters who worked with her, the donors would stop donating. That's why it was utterly important that they had confidence in the cowboys moving forward and in his leadership.

Keeping the ranch alive without the help of donors was a dream of Randy's. While his aunt had the support of wealthy people in the riding world, he dreamed of making it independent. Mayisha had created a model that was easy for wealthy donors to buy into, and their support had helped sustain a youth equestrian program for young black children in one of the most impoverished cities in the United States. It was a symbiotic relationship that potentially leaned toward white guilt—giving generously to young black children made many of the donors feel good about their own lives.

When the Compton Cowboys took over, however, it was obvious that they weren't the children of yesteryear. The boys who had grown up going to the donors' ranches to learn how to ride and spend time in communities outside of Compton had turned into black men. And donors didn't see black men as safe investments, the way they did black children.

Having young black men at the helm of the ranch operation instilled doubt and worry and fear in the hearts of many of the donors. They doubted their ability to continue running the ranch, and Mayisha's concerns about image only compounded the donors' reluctance. It felt like the world was against the cowboys, and that made them become more insular. If the ranch was going to survive, it was going to be because of the cowboys. They were going to have to rely on themselves.

FIVE MEN WORKED tirelessly all morning to install a large outdoor tent that covered most of the riding area. They had been working for hours until one of them realized that some of the support ropes were missing. After an hour, and after various phone calls, another worker decided to head back to the office to pick up the ropes that should have been brought that morning.

"None of that would have happened on my watch," Mayisha thought to herself while observing the fiasco from the driver's seat of her truck.

As the founder and director of the Compton Jr. Posse, she had run the organization with a combination of tough love mixed with sporadic moments of tenderness and affection that were felt but hardly seen. Her brand of tough love was often the only defense against the neighborhood gangs with whom she competed for new recruits. She had to provide the same things they did in order to keep children interested: safety and a sense of belonging.

Mayisha was also in competition with a rap group that made recruiting horse riders challenging. The rise of local Compton gangster rap group Niggaz Wit Attitudes, or N.W.A, natives of Compton and South Central, helped usher in a new image for Compton while she was opening the ranch. While she tried to keep her kids off the streets by preaching a gospel of horse riding, the messages of N.W.A songs like "Fuck tha Police" and "Gangsta Gangsta" promoted the life that she was fighting against.

If Compton was already stigmatized around the world as a

haven for crime and violence, N.W.A further crystallized deep-seated fears of gun-toting young black youth. None of this made Mayisha's job any easier. The children of the neighborhood had to decide between the version of Compton that N.W.A was describing and the Compton she wanted to create. It was a battle that she often lost.

Mayisha continued her drive to the hardware store, in search of an assortment of rocks to fill up the fifty glass vases that she had purchased to place on the tables. The party also required palm trees to go along with the party theme.

It would be their very last time at the ranch for a lot of her friends and family. The same people who had helped her accomplish her dream of maintaining one of the only black ranches west of the Mississippi—a reliable team of donors, philanthropists, and community leaders—were also aging and running out of the energy and resources to keep it afloat.

Since she had moved away to Norco, her connection to the ranch had changed. Fewer children showed up to learn how to ride on the weekends and the program that she had started for her children and their friends began to lose its allure.

Driving through the farms only confirmed what she already knew: the community had drastically changed since she first moved to Caldwell Street over thirty years ago. The black children and families playing in the streets and walking to and from local schools were replaced by Latino schoolchildren who walked in groups of at least five or six with young mothers who pushed strollers and walked close behind them. Even the black garbage collectors who had picked up the ranch's trash were replaced by brown faces.

As a former real estate broker, Mayisha knew the housing

market and understood why African-American families had begun to move out. As more and more African-American families moved to cities like San Bernardino, Fontana, and Ontario, Mexican families began moving in and living in homes where multiple family incomes offset the rising costs of housing. Some Compton residents, as well as local public officials, saw this as an attempt to force black families out of the community, which created racial strife that began at the political level and eventually trickled down to the schools.

"Taco Tuesday" wasn't a day where people ate Mexican food in Compton. For many years, it meant the day of the week when black teenagers would pick fights with Mexicans in schoolyards throughout the city. "Punch a Mexican Friday" was also a popular day.

Even as a staunch pro-black thinker and supporter of the Nation of Islam, Mayisha never subscribed to the politics of division that plagued her community. She understood the factors that drove Latino families to Compton. She had created the Junior Posse for all the children of the farms, and as time passed, that meant more Latinos.

"WHERE'S YOUR FATHER?" Mayisha asked a Latino teenager who was helping load up the back of a truck with brown dirt in front of Jose's house. She put her truck in park and waited on the right side of the street. "He said he would be here to help me get some palm trees."

The boy stopped what he was doing and walked into the house to look for Jose.

Moments later, the front door swung open and Jose stepped

out with a phone next to his ear, wearing a blue T-shirt and grey work pants with splashes of different-colored paint on them. His scruffy demeanor was offset by a pleasant smile.

"Hola, Mayisha," he said while hanging up his phone, placing it in his front shirt pocket.

"How are you, Jose?" Mayisha asked in a joyful tone from inside her truck. "How's the wife?"

"My wife?" he asked while laughing hysterically and looking to his left and right to make sure she wasn't around. "Oh, I let her go," he said in a heavy accent accentuated by long, thoughtful pauses between his words.

"You let her go?" Mayisha responded, shocked. "What did you do with her?"

"I sent her to Mexico for a very long time. It was getting too expensive to keep her around, you know?"

The two laughed and smiled. The old friends hadn't seen one another since she moved to Norco. They had worked together on numerous occasions over the years. Seeing people like Jose reminded her of the beauty and hardship that had come with the organization she founded. The success of the ranch relied on the relationships she had formed with people like Jose who lived in the farms, relationships built on respect and trust and guided by a language of love.

"Well, I came here for those palms that we spoke about on the phone this morning. If you happen to find any, bring them over to the ranch. I have to go buy some rocks for some vases right now, but just drop them over there if you find any. And come to my party, your whole family is invited," she added while putting her car in gear and beginning to drive off.

"Okay, Mayisha, that sounds good," he said. "I'll let you know what I find." He returned to a conversation on his phone, seamlessly switching back into Spanish.

As she began to shift her car into drive, an older-model Chevy Camaro drove up to the left side of her car playing loud Mexican banda music. A long metal crutch hung from the window.

"Is that you, Guero?" Mayisha said to herself as the car approached.

"Hi, Mayisha. You like my music? It's your CD!" explained a fair-skinned Mexican man with blue eyes while holding on to his crutch with one hand and the steering wheel with the other hand. His daughter sat in the passenger seat, looking down at her phone while the loud music blared out of his speakers and into the neighborhood.

"That is not my music, man!" she said with a large smile, followed by a short laugh. "You're crazy!"

Guero spoke to Mayisha about a five-year-old mare that he couldn't ride anymore since he broke his leg a few months earlier. "I'll sell it for a few hundred," he said. "I don't care, I just want to get rid of it."

Mayisha agreed to ask around to see if anyone was interested.

"Take your CD before you go," Guero said as he ejected the CD that he was playing and handed it to Mayisha.

As she took the CD and placed it in her dashboard, Mayisha said, "Bye, Guero!"

Jose and Guero had been her friends for years. Both of their families had also owned horses and had worked together on numerous occasions. When Mayisha needed sand for her stalls and they had extra, they would drop it off at the ranch free of cost. When she had extra sand, she would do the same. Every horse-owning family on the farms worked in synchronicity, regardless of their race. They were part of a unique horse-riding community and spoke a language of softness and kindness only understood from inside the confines of the ranch.

Life had hardened some aspects of Mayisha, but if you caught her on the right day at the right time, you would find her laughing full-body laughs. It was part of the reason why people loved and trusted her. She had the ability to speak to anyone, and her intimate relationships with people throughout Compton were a testament to that.

Her hand remained outside the truck as she waved to pedestrians and cars alike. She knew most of them by first name. Sometimes she would drive around and people would walk up to her and call her "Mom." She wouldn't recognize them at first, but would then realize they were once a part of the CJP.

There was another side to Mayisha, though. The severity of the times sometimes required a sterner approach than she would have liked. Many of the children whom she brought to the ranch came from single-parent homes. Responsibility and discipline were hard to come by and not something that was readily enforced. She'd learned how to show kids tough love, knowing they wouldn't survive otherwise.

She expected excellence and a full commitment from each CJP rider in ways that some children could not handle, leading to frequent falling-outs with children and families and conflict with community and political organizations.

At one point she decided to switch up the riding styles, opting to leave western-style for English-style riding. Western saddles were heavier and larger than English saddles and were primarily designed as a way to spread the weight over a larger area of the horse, making longer rides more comfortable. English saddles, in contrast, were designed to give the rider closer contact to the horse when jumping.

But changing the style of riding did more than make riders adjust the size of their saddles. It eventually changed the demographics of the program.

Western-style riding provided an outlet for aggression and anger for many of the young people who rode with the Junior Posse. Western riders rode fast and hard and prided themselves on their aggressive approach. English-style riding was more formal, more restrained and European, and it didn't have a history of black riders like western-style riding did. If western riding was a way to recover a forgotten history, English-style riding almost had the opposite effect. Western riding created the same feeling that many of the youth felt after a big hit on the football field—it became an outlet and a form of therapy. When the styles of riding changed, that feeling was gone, and as a result, so were most of the kids. They were asked to dress differently: denim jeans, white T-shirts, and cowboy hats were exchanged for black helmets, knee-high boots, dark jackets, and polo shirts. Some of the kids who needed the program more than anyone left after refusing to ride English and were eventually lost to the streets.

For Mayisha, changing riding styles was intended to secure more funding from wealthy donors for whom the fancier English style was more culturally acceptable. Western-style riding wasn't as lucrative as English was, and Mayisha believed that the ranch would be able to attract more donors and resources. She never imagined it would deter kids from joining. She never imagined the result would be a life-or-death situation for some of her riders.

"WHERE IS MY wallet?" Mayisha was frantically searching through a pile of receipts and empty coffee cups inside her truck while parked at the McDonald's drive-thru. Her vehicle was a haven for miscellaneous items like receipts and paperwork that had piled up since she bought it.

"There it is." She leaned out the window to speak into the drive-thru intercom. "I'll have two burritos and a coffee, please."

At this point in her life, her health had been ailing. She had gained some weight and was no longer the energetic woman that she had been required to be most of her life. Running the ranch had taken a deep toll on her body over the years. Just two years earlier she had suffered through a mild stroke that left her bedridden for almost a month. She had since slowly eased her way into the background of the ranch's daily operations.

Like other black families during the war years, the Hook family arrived at Harbor City with the hope of working in war industry jobs available to African-Americans. They were lured from Oklahoma with the promise of a better life, a chance to live outside of the bounds of a racially restrictive community. They believed in the dream of California, and Mayisha's mother found work as a cook for several healthy family initiatives. Her father was a World War II veteran who worked on the railroads after the war. After Mayisha graduated from Loyola Marymount University, she immediately began working in real estate. Her career advanced and soon she was known as one of the savviest Realtors in Los Angeles.

But while her career ascended, something about her life felt like it was missing. One day while she was scouting for properties, a client of hers recommended that she have a look at the Richland Farms. There's farmland and horses, they said, and it's right in the middle of Compton. Raising her children near a big plot of land where animals roamed freely had always been a dream of hers. The stories her father had shared with her, vivid memories of his days as a child growing up on a farm in the Oklahoma countryside, flashed through her head.

She cherished memories of watching westerns with her father every Saturday morning, even though it upset her that there were never black people in them. Her father would get so happy when the Native Americans would beat the white soldiers, feeling a sense of kinship with them even though he was once in the military.

The children who showed up to Mayisha's makeshift ranch had also never seen black cowboys on their television screens. They never read about the proud history of black cowboys in the founding of the American West. They were never taught about the ingenuity of cowboys like Nat Love, who was born a slave in Tennessee in 1854, freed at the conclusion of the Civil War, and gained prominence throughout the Southwest as a trusted guide and showman. Or Bill Pickett, one of the West's most famous rodeo champions and actors, who would later be inducted into the Pro Rodeo Hall of Fame. Cowboys, the children believed, were white and only looked like John Wayne or Clint Eastwood, both famous for their roles in western films that depicted them as victors in ruthless gunfights against Native Americans. So when young black children began to ride horses on Caldwell it changed the neighborhood and their lives forever.

The new generation of cowboys, led by her nephew Randy, however, worried Mayisha. She had raised the cowboys under a strict moral code, one that she had learned when she converted to Islam in the 1980s, following the teachings of Minister Louis Farrakhan of the Nation of Islam. Minister Farrakhan's message of black pride and self-reliance impressed her, and after meeting her first husband, she converted to Islam and changed her last name to Akbar.

Being a member of the Nation of Islam continued to guide Mayisha's life, and the cowboys, she believed, were in danger of living up to some of the damaging stereotypes that she had tried so hard to combat.

She was concerned about her nephew's group now taking the reins of the ranch. She felt they were at risk of representing thuggery and not giving back to the kids. They needed to be better role models. They would constantly tell her she was "old school," but in her heart, she felt that some of the old ways were more wholesome. She needed her successors to understand how detrimental their image could be for their culture—black cowboy culture.

Her biggest concern for the eventual transition of the ranch was the way the cowboys carried themselves. As members of the Compton Junior Posse, they were never allowed to ride in anything but the blue CJP shirts they had been given. They were never allowed to ride shirtless or with anything but crisp riding boots. Members of the cowboys like Kenneth, notorious for riding without a shirt, had the potential, she believed, to undo so much of the work she had given so much of her life to create, to undermine the reputation of the cowboys.

Still, while she had qualms about the direction that the cowboys were embarking on, she understood that in a few days the ranch would no longer be hers. It felt like letting a child go off to college with the realization that he or she might never return home again. Mayisha understood that her nephew and the guys working on the ranch had to take the reins, that she had to trust them to do a good job. But she hoped they would see the bigger picture, in particular how they would lead the next generation of kids.

She wished she'd never had the stroke—perhaps it would have

allowed the Junior Posse's board members to continue to believe in her ability to run the ranch the way she used to. They believed that the funding—almost thirty thousand dollars a month, with extensive fund-raising—would be a challenge without her, because she was a fearless fund-raiser. On top of an uncanny wit, it was her charm and ability to connect with people that proved effective.

But there was only one Mayisha, and finding someone to replace her was almost unimaginable. She often thought back to the days when she first started the Compton Junior Posse in 1988, and how far they had come since—the trips that sponsored her riders around the world, the college scholarships that the organization provided, and the lives she had saved over the years. With her retirement, she had decided to close the operation down for one year, until Randy started talking about how they could potentially make an income for the organization.

Mayisha had mixed feelings about the cowboys' reliance on striking it rich through entertainment. She was no stranger to the entertainment industry and had been approached by dozens of production companies and Hollywood studios over the years to develop films about the CJP. The deals seemed lucrative, but she was more interested in preserving the integrity of the organization's image. She worried that the cowboys had delusions of grandeur and didn't quite understand the nature of the entertainment business.

She tried to manage their expectations, tried to teach them the value of being patient and putting in the hard work—eventually the industry would come to them. If she'd learned anything as a handler of the ranch, it was that hard work was hard for a reason.

THE FIRES

WHILE CONCERNS ABOUT THE FUTURE of the ranch continued to boil on the farms, Charles Harris was able to momentarily escape them on his drives to his training sessions in Malibu.

He turned up the volume in his car a little louder than usual and played smooth R&B while the dark blue Pacific Ocean water reflected outside the left driver's-side door. To his right were the Santa Monica bluffs, one of the first places where he took the mother of his children on a date. A photo of Bayley and Blake, his two children, was stuck to his dashboard with an old piece of gum, a reminder of why he was making the hour-and-a-half drive up the Pacific Coast Highway to Malibu in the first place.

Meanwhile, a driver in a shiny pearl-white convertible Mercedes-Benz attempted to pass him, but failed. The car sped up and failed again, this time almost causing an accident on the highway. The Mercedes finally passed him minutes later and honked at Charles as the back of his California license plate got smaller and smaller as he sped ahead.

Charles was unbothered by the driver's rage. Perhaps it was the effects of the 'wood that he had smoked with Carlton earlier on the ranch. Or maybe it was the life lessons he had learned in the past two years after a mishap with the law that landed him in jail for a couple nights.

The Pacific Coast Highway was busier than normal for a Thursday afternoon. The arduous drive from Compton to Malibu on a weekly basis had become routine for Felicia Jones's eldest son.

He was the pride and joy of the family and an Olympic hopeful with big dreams. Training to become the first African-American hunter jumper required hours upon hours of hard work and dedication. Since the beginning of the year, however, finding the time to jump didn't come as easy as it used to. Sponsors and supporters began to dwindle as the costs of competitive jumping continued to increase.

What began as a daily drive to Suze's home in the Malibu hills declined to only three times a week, and eventually to only one training session per week. The less time he spent training, the more weight he gained, and the less smooth his jumps became. The uncanny timing that he had been known for in the equestrian community was slowly beginning to slip before his eyes.

On top of that, working as a part-time construction worker and a stocker at Walmart squeezed the minutes out of each of his days. Every hour that he clocked in to work felt like an hour that took him further away from the dream that he had first imagined when he began jumping as a fourteen-year-old. At twenty-seven, the dream seemed more unattainable than ever.

He pulled off the Pacific Coast Highway and made a right onto a dirt road that eventually led to the ranch of Susan, a supporter of the Junior Posse whom he had known for years. His tires skidded on the loose gravel, leaving a growing trail of dust behind as he continued up the mountain.

For someone who had been born and raised in Compton, driving through nature was cathartic and removed him from the dangers that he had experienced in his neighborhood. Every time he drove to Susan's ranch he was transported into a world where green brush and wildlife outnumbered the humans and cars he was used to being around. It was an escape, a world that wasn't dictated by the black-and-white uniforms of police officers, or the black skin of young men in his neighborhood who were often shot at by the same officers. This world was green, and its natural soundscape overpowered the sounds coming from his car's speakers and the low murmur of the traffic on the Pacific Coast Highway miles below.

Susan's home was the farthest from the highway and required driving along several dirt roads before reaching her property. The entrance felt familiar at this point. He had made the drive so many times before that it began to feel like muscle memory—the same way he used to shoot free throws with his eyes closed in high school to impress the prettiest girls on campus. Pulling off into the dirt road was his favorite part of the drive because it allowed his mind to zone out and everything he worried about to come into crystal-clear focus: his children, his family, and their future.

Charles parked his car, got out, and took a long whiff of the fresh Malibu air, picking up the scent of the gardenias and roses in the nearby garden.

"Hi, Charles," Susan said with a smile, welcoming him inside her home. "Are you hungry?" Charles smiled and said that he was.

It was routine for them to eat and study the equestrian books that she had bought for him years before. He studied the books with an intensity that he had never approached his schoolwork with. Studying diligently and reading about new training methods from the best equestrian jumpers was the only way to improve his jumping, and there were tips in the books that he hadn't learned on the farms.

An hour later, Charles and Susan headed down to the stables to groom and saddle up two Thoroughbred horses that poked their heads out from the stalls as they approached them. Warm

Blood, Charles's favorite horse, neighed and flicked his tail at the sight of them.

Warm Blood stood still while he brushed his long brown coat, occasionally flipping his mane in the air. Charles had never owned his own horse, but grooming Warm Blood felt like the closest thing he had to owning his own. "Good horse," he said. "Good horse." After thirty minutes, the two hopped on their horses and rode around the local trails before training.

Although Charles's jumping timing had declined over the past year, the intensity that he brought to each of his training sessions hadn't. The first hour of training included flatwork—a series of slow trots over poles on the ground that loosened up the horses before jumping. "Groundwork," as Charles also called it, was as important as jumping because it let him feel out what kind of mood the horse was in that day. If the horse was having a bad day, it would tense up when Charles pulled on its reins. If it was calm and rested, it would comply with each tug of the reins. The second hour included jumping and working on perfecting the two-point jumping position.

Charles crouched on his horse and got ready for the first big jump of the day. He bent his knees in a forty-five-degree angle and lifted his bottom off the horse's back as the horse timed its jump and sailed over the wooden pole with ease, landing moments later while Charles's body hovered closely over its back.

He rode toward the next jump. One stride, two strides, just like he had done for the past fifteen years of his life, and Warm Blood was in the air again. His body leaned forward on the second jump, prompting a response from Susan, who stood feet away.

"Make sure you let the horse's feet relax on the landing," she said while looking intently at him. "And keep your knees bent a little more next time."

As a jumper it was Charles's job to ensure that his horse was comfortable with every leap. Horses like Warm Blood had been trained their entire lives to jump and just needed the reassurance to make the hurdles. Charles admired the power of the horse when it approached the jump—he could feel the horse's strength building up, knowing it wanted to get over the obstacle. But it was important for him to keep rhythm with Warm Blood to help him make that jump, together.

He landed his jumps the rest of the afternoon, leaving a big smile on Susan's face.

CHARLES FELT CONFLICTED when news came that Mayisha would no longer be running the ranch at the end of the year. He had been one of CJP's most successful jumpers and one of the program's stars. When other members of the CJP pushed back against switching to English-style riding, Charles was one of the few riders who welcomed the change with open arms. Mayisha was the first person to introduce him to show jumping and the first to help him realize that he could make a career out of it. But because show jumping required the most resources and training, it almost meant that Charles would have to find creative ways to fund his training. None of his closest friends knew how to ride English, so he had to rely on wealthy riders to show him the ropes—it would be his only hope for survival.

As a twenty-seven-year-old, the names and faces had changed, but the same wealthy white horse riders continued to help. Each trainer—Nicole, Tobias, Will—had seen the same potential in him that led him to believe that he could become an Olympian. But the same issues arose with nearly every single one of them. After a while, they all wanted to be compensated for their time and for using their horses. The promise of Charles striking it rich in a competitive show jumping circuit wasn't enough for them to continue to support him.

But making the Olympics was still Charles's dream, and it had more to do with his community than it did with him.

He really wanted to show kids from the 'hood that you didn't have to be a gangster or sell drugs. He could remember how in the early days of riding, he didn't want to wear his britches out in public because he felt ashamed. It took years to shed that embarrassment. Now, after all these years of hard work, he didn't give a damn. Trainers may come and go, horses too, but he wore his britches every day. It was a part of him now.

Daily training at Susan's continued for the next few months. His timing was improving and his landings, always his lowest set of scores, were smoothing out. The next competition was months away and the progress he was making impressed everyone on the ranch.

One morning he received a call from Susan describing an ongoing issue that had recently arisen at the ranch. She explained that the property was in the middle of a tough legal battle with a pair of local residents who were concerned that the horses she owned were damaging their property. The city of Malibu got involved and she was being sued for large amounts of money. She wasn't going down without a fight, she assured Charles, who remained silent on the phone. The phone call was reminiscent of the one that he had received late at night the previous November when Nicole, one of his trainers, called to explain that she could no longer train him because she was going to be incarcerated for a car accident that had left one person dead and another critically injured. Or a different trainer who eventually told him he couldn't train with him anymore because his rate was too high and Charles could no longer afford him.

He hung up the phone with Susan and burst into tears. Just when all the stars had begun to align in his favor, when his timing was getting back to where it once was, something else would come up to destroy his plans.

Wealthy white people with kind hearts had always taken a liking to Charles, a black boy from Compton. They had been the reason for his development as a jumper since he first joined the CJP. He was their favorite. His full-toothed grin, handsome features, and pleasant disposition quelled any deep-seated fears they may have had about black people. Giving back to black boys and girls from the 'hood like Charles was a way to reconcile their thirst for charity and absolve themselves, he believed, from any sense of guilt they may have had about racism.

But at the end of the day, they still had control over his dream and were armed with the power to take it away at any moment. He felt vulnerable. Naked, even. It felt like his black body was being dangled on a string while wealthy white people toyed with his life.

Driving back to the ranch after the call, he knew he needed to get more support. To find the right people to back him up. To find somebody, anybody, to believe in him enough.

Being rejected from the ranch was the last straw for Charles. It also coincided with the troubles he had begun to experience with Koya, the mother of his two children. When the two had first met near the farms more than seven years earlier, they were instantly drawn to each other. After courting for a few weeks, they began dating, and the pair soon became inseparable. Charles loved that Koya lived down the street from the ranch. He could ride horses and see her on the same day. It was the perfect setup. But things changed after they had Bayley, their daughter, and then Blake. When they moved in with Charles's mother in Palmdale, Koya felt isolated from her family and friends in Compton. As the months passed, they began to spend more time apart than together.

A few years later they were fully separated and living in different parts of the city. Koya had filed to have full custody of Bayley, who was now six, and Blake, who was four. In the meantime, Charles was only allowed to see his children on weekend visits. He was now separated from his children and from the horses that could provide for him and his family.

Court visits became the norm. During one visit, Charles lost control and began yelling at both Koya and the judge. He was later sentenced for contempt, but the charges were eventually dropped. The time that he did spend with his children was spent at malls and parks around the area. Even if he couldn't see them as often as he would have liked, he was going to make sure they wore the nicest things. He bought them Jordan basketball shoes and sweatsuits even though Charles believed Koya returned them to exchange them for money. To support himself and his family, he took a job working at Walmart as an overnight stocker. A few months later, his brother Rambo joined him. Together, they unloaded pallets from trucks and stocked aisles with spatulas, knives, and coffee makers from late at night into the early hours of the morning. It wasn't the life he had imagined for himself, but it kept him afloat and allowed him to purchase things for his children.

In November, Charles had begun thinking about making a comeback into the sport. He was flipping through the channels when he stumbled on news of a raging fire that was quickly spreading throughout Malibu. The fire had already killed two people and was on the path to destroying thousands of acres of land, charring and blackening the same soil where he used to practice his jumping. He watched the television as the fires burned, knowing that his dreams were also burning to the ground as more and more structures were destroyed. He had been meaning to pick up his phone to call Susan, but without an arena to practice on, the phone call would be futile. If things had seemed bleak for Charles prior to the fires, his dream of becoming an Olympic champion now seemed more unattainable than ever.

THE ART OF PEER PRESSURE

ONE OF BYRON'S SHOELACES DRAGGED behind him as he walked down Caldwell in a faded black T-shirt and baggy blue jeans. Tiny beads of sweat began to collect on his forehead, but his eyes remained fixed on the ground beneath him as the sun beat down on his body. He only looked up when a car passed him, hoping to see a familiar face inside.

In the old days, Byron would have recognized every car that drove down Caldwell, but with the changing of the neighborhood and his CD business gone, he felt like he hardly knew anyone these days. The fast-paced Mexican music that played from inside most of the cars was completely foreign to his ears. Only a few of the Mexican horse riders who had been friends with Mayisha greeted him as they rode past him on finely groomed white Friesians. The sound of their hooves faded away as they walked in the opposite direction.

Almost an hour earlier, a group of Mexican mothers had rushed their children to school wearing house slippers and sweatpants, hoping to beat the 8 a.m. bell that signaled the start of their children's school day. By the time they dropped their children off that morning, Byron had already been walking around the farms for a couple of hours.

He walked on Alondra Boulevard, toward Acacia, stopping at the gas station to ask for change—the same gas station where Black had been murdered six months ago. "You got fifty cents?" he asked a few different people that morning. One person gave him a quarter, another a few dimes; most ignored him. After spending an hour there, he made his way to the canals to visit a group of homeless people whom he had befriended over the last few months.

Byron sat down on an upside-down white bucket and watched the group while they drank alcohol out of brown paper bags near a batch of fresh hoof marks that the cowboys had left on the canal trail earlier that week. A few men sat with their backs against the wall, taking advantage of the shade it provided them from the harsh Compton sun.

One of the people in the group, a husky black man with a buried scar under his right eye, wore a two-toned durag on his head. He straightened out a blue tarp similar to the one that Mr. Sanchez had used to protect his taco stand from the rain. He carefully draped it across two shopping carts filled with bottles, cans, and pieces of scrap metal that he had been collecting, forming a home encampment. A vintage light blue Compton High letterman's jacket with the name "Johnson" embroidered across the left breast—his most prized possession—lay on the ground, eagerly awaiting the return of the Friday night stadium lights that lit up his nearby Compton High alma mater once a week.

A woman who had recently joined the group caught Byron's attention. She was white and from the Midwest and had spent years lost in the underworld of heroin addiction and prostitution in downtown Los Angeles's Skid Row. She had moved to Compton earlier in the year to follow a boyfriend who had since abandoned her for another woman. Most of the neighborhood's heroin trade had historically been controlled by the Acacia Crips but had since been taken over by the Compton Varrio 70's, one of the deadliest Mexican gangs in the area, who offered their product at a cheaper price than what she had been paying in the streets of downtown Los Angeles. The mysterious woman with wide Caribbean blue eyes reminded him of some of the actresses in the old cowboy westerns that he had watched as a child. At one point during her youth the sun had shone on her long blond hair, but now it was dull and lifeless from months without bathing. Byron shyly smiled at her while she injected her arm with heroin that within moments had entirely disappeared into a protruding blue vein deep into her frail left arm. He watched her as she closed her eyes and fell asleep next to the letterman's jacket, leaving Byron and the rest of the group alone with their thoughts.

Byron walked back to the ranch and arrived at the same time as Layton, who parked his shiny dark blue Lexus sedan next to Anthony's truck, barely missing the same mailbox that had been knocked down too many times to count over the years.

"Hey man you g-g-got fifty cents?" Byron quickly asked Layton with an outstretched hand as he got out of his car.

Like the rest of the cowboys, Layton had known Byron his entire life and remembered the days when Byron would give him and his friends CDs or buy them sodas and candy from the liquor store. He was one of the few cowboys who almost always reached into his pocket to give Byron money whenever he asked.

"What up, Byron?" Layton asked him, pulling out a wrinkled dollar. He handed it to him.

Byron's eyes widened as he grabbed the dollar. "Thanks, man," he said without a stammer as the two walked to the back of the ranch where several of the cowboys had been hanging out.

They walked to an area that hadn't physically changed as much as their bodies had in the last thirty years. The large riding arena, fifteen-horse stables, and thirty-foot-high barn were still stacked with hay and ranch equipment. A trailer that hadn't been used in years now served as a storage space for reins and other tack. On one side inside the barn's walls were several dry-erase boards where Anthony was able to keep track of the horses' health and their feeding times.

It was Anthony and Terrance's birthday and several of the guys had gathered inside the toolshed to listen to music and avoid the heat. Charles and Carlton were busy playing a dice game while Keenan watched diligently, egging both of them on as the dice continued to roll different sets of numbers, prompting different responses from the group.

"Snake eyes!" Charles yelled.

Anthony and Terrance sat back and watched the game from nearby chairs. The pair had known one another for as long as they could remember, and celebrating their birthdays together had become a tradition since Anthony was released from prison more than twelve years earlier. Though they were both in their midthirties, the years had been extremely kind to them. At thirty-six, Anthony had only a few grey hairs beginning to show on his head. Terrance hadn't changed much at all. He still had the same long slender face and dark brown skin free of wrinkles, and he continued to prefer the flashy fashion choices that he had been known for on the farms for years. At six feet six inches tall, he continued to be mistaken for a basketball player.

When they were born, the city of Compton was known as one of the world's most dangerous communities. Unemployment was almost twice the national average and social and political neglect led to the rise of organized street crime and gangs throughout the city. Murder rates skyrocketed, and the school system nearly crumbled due to mismanagement as the allocation of resources shifted out of the city. Many of the middle-class black families that had formed the backbone of the city moved out, creating a "black exodus." By the mid-1980s, the crack cocaine epidemic had emerged, devastating the city and all of its inhabitants. Anthony and Terrance were both born in a generation where babies were often exposed to crack cocaine in utero.

Layton wore a crisp Barcelona soccer jersey and a black baseball cap with white Apple earbuds. His beard had grown over the fall, and with winter approaching, there was more incentive to grow it out. Since he had begun to work at an electronic appliance store, he spent less time on the ranch than ever. Earlier in the year, when his only source of income was producing beats for local rappers, he lived in between the Hook residence, a girlfriend's house, and Kenneth's back house that doubled as a bedroom and makeshift recording studio. His son, now in elementary school, lived close by and split time with the family of his mother, who had died suddenly years earlier.

When he wasn't bragging about how much he could outride everyone else in the group, Layton was quick with a joke. Like with Charles, his jokes had no boundaries. Anyone could be a victim.

While the front of the ranch was quiet, the back was buzzing with more energy than usual. Music blasted on the speaker system. Shots of tequila and lit backwoods were passed back and forth while a few of the horses wandered around the arena. As the eldest members of the cowboys, Anthony and Terrance had survived some of its toughest times together. Through gang wars, dirt bike riding accidents, and the deaths of close friends, the two had formed an inseparable bond.

Terrance, the tallest member of the group, was also its most reserved. He never really seemed rattled by anything, a perfect fit to the stereotype about people from the West Coast being super laid-back. He spoke slowly and with a slight southern twang inherited from his grandparents. His calm demeanor had helped him learn to ride horses as an eight-year-old in his uncle's driveway. It was also what helped him recover from multiple falls when his older friends first took him riding around the neighborhood. As the youngest one in the group back then, he always remained the quietest. He'd discovered at an early age that he learned more when he stayed quiet and observed.

Terrance thought about Black, who had been murdered in 2004. Black was one of the people who taught him and Anthony how to ride, and as the horses trotted around the arena, his friend's absence weighed heavy on his mind.

The Sunday he was murdered, Terrance and Black and a few other friends had been cruising up and down the Crenshaw Boulevard strip all evening. When the skies darkened, the friends decided to call it a night and Black dropped each of them off at their homes. Terrance was the last one to get dropped off, unaware that it would be the last goodbye they would ever have. Black drove on to the Acacia gas station to refuel his car and minutes later lay bleeding to death on the street. Witnesses claim that within minutes of his arrival a group of unidentified men had engaged in a verbal altercation with him, which ended in a shooting.

"You tryna take a shot?" Layton asked Terrance, after filling up a shot glass with tequila and pouring it down his throat. Terrance snapped out of his daze and looked at Anthony. A smile emerged.

"Damn, peer pressure is a mothafucka. Fuck it, why not?" Terrance calmly said.

"Shit, it's both of y'all birthday, I'm a go to the store and get us something more to drink on," Layton said while making his way to the front of the ranch.

"Yo, it's also my birthday too, nigga," Keenan shouted from beyond the fence, smiling. "Don't forget about me."

THE RANCH WAS more than a place to ride horses. For nearly all the members of the cowboys, as well as other members of the community, it was an ecosystem that gave everyone in it meaning and a way to preserve their friendships. Over the years, some of its elements had changed. The ten-foot-high basketball hoop that provided the backdrop for some of the most intense three-on-three games in Compton had been taken down, and the driveway was now home to a few older-model cars that had not been driven in years. Before everyone had horse dreams, each member of the cowboys, like others who grew up in Compton during the peak of the Los Angeles Lakers' showtime days, had hoop dreams. But as everyone grew older and busier, the games slowly began to decrease.

The difference between the world inside the ranch and that outside of it was stark. Inside was a sanctuary where everyone came to find balance and peace. Hanging out and smoking 'woods and drinking could have easily gotten them arrested or fined had they been doing that outside on the porch. But inside the world of the ranch, there were different sets of rules. At the ranch, there was a protective barrier between their flesh and the hot pieces of metal that shot out of the Nutty Blocc's guns. Keenan and Layton had been chased back to the farms too many times to count, and each time they cleared it to the ranch, they knew they would survive. It was their safe haven.

The horses on the ranch had arrived in different ways. Most were bought at auctions for throwaway and abused animals. They were horses that other riders and racers had given up on. They were abused, malnourished, and if they came from racetracks, they were frequently on their last legs. They were sometimes bought for two hundred dollars and nursed back to life. Other horses were donated by riders who believed in the Compton Junior Posse and Compton Cowboys.

Like the throwaway horses that filled the ranch, each member of the Compton Cowboys had at one point in their lives been given up on at an early age. Black boys and girls like them were born into a world where the color of their skin served as a scathing reminder of difference and erasure. They were born into worlds that never gave blackness the chance to be cowboys and cowboys the chance to be black.

As time passed, these same children grew into full-fledged cowboys who developed inseparable bonds with their horses. Horses opened spaces for love to reemerge, a love that the streets had once taken away. The horses listened when nobody else would and showed up when nobody else did. They cared for them devotedly, and in return the horses taught them how to love.

Slowly, hardened glares turned into smiles. Layers upon layers of pain and setback began to dissolve. The horses brought joy with them, and it took up permanent residence in their hearts. The horses, they witnessed, had the ability to turn the most aggressive gangster on the block into the sweetest version of who they were as small children. Kind. Quiet, even. Every horse ride brought the cowboys closer to spreading this same feeling to members of their families who continued to fight a war inside and outside of their homes, a war that almost always involved violence and addiction. Loving their horses helped them love themselves and those in their community, and though every throwaway horse was once heading to death, in the end, the horses saved them, too.

MOST CONVERSATIONS IN the back of the ranch revolved around weed, money, women, and horses. Music played loudly from an aux cord that was connected to someone's phone, providing the soundtrack for a series of ongoing debates between the guys. The ranch was also a place where information about the world was passed on and discussed. Local politics, government, technology, and finances were talked about with a clarity and intellect that television political pundits only aspired to reach. Everyone contributed to conversations and to a tradition that predated every member of the Compton Cowboys.

The culture of black urban cowboys came directly from the mythology created by the cowboys of the American West. At one point in the early history of the West, one in four cowboys were black. When the frontier was being settled in the nineteenth century, white slave owners moved out west to states like Texas with their slaves. They relied on enslaved black men and women to herd cattle and care for the land. When the Civil War ended, freed African-Americans often continued as paid cowhands, cashing in on their skills at a time when there were very few options for black employment. Cowboys like Nat Love, born in 1854 in Tennessee, helped establish a tradition that became influential in the founding of the West. In the eyes of black cowboys like Love, the West was a place of reinvention, free from the racial inequities of the South.

This was also an era when the emergence of the Buffalo Soldiers helped shape the West. Regiments of African-American cavalry created shortly after Congress passed the 1866 Army Reorganization Act, they helped establish order on the frontier and were particularly entrusted with the duty of controlling the Native Americans of the Great Plains. The Buffalo Soldiers were also instrumental in protecting national park land and fighting wildfires in California parks like Yosemite and Sequoia.

The stories that black cowboys created were used as a way to endure long and cold nights on the prairies of the Great Plains or the deserts of the Southwest. Black cowboys lived hard, rugged lives that fostered intimate connections with the horses they rode.

Like the cowboys who once roamed the western frontier during the nineteenth century, the Compton Cowboys were also keen on survival tactics. The streets taught them how to escape danger and who not to trust. They knew they had a better chance of surviving on their horses than they did on foot.

The cowboys of the old West were safer on horses because they had a higher vantage point over their surroundings and could escape dangerous situations at a gallop. Horses could sense danger and alert riders beforehand. At times the horses themselves even became the armor during deadly shootouts or a barrier against harsh weather conditions.

Similarly, for the black cowboys of the Richland Farms, *not* riding your horse could mean the difference between life and death. On foot, black men, like the cowboys, were stereotyped both by the police and by opposing gangs. The police profiled black men in different ways: a black man on a horse was almost always considered less dangerous than one on foot. At this point in their life, walking to the store wasn't worth the time and hassle of getting physically harassed by the police. Each cowboy knew the risks. Gangsters, too, had their biases. Black men on horses weren't as threatening and often got a pass.

In the old West, cowboys were only fearful of bands of renegade outlaws and Native American tribes who fought tirelessly to protect their lands. The danger that the cowboys faced in Compton, in contrast, was warring neighborhood gangs and unlawful police.

A CONVERSATION BETWEEN Keenan and Terrance took place in between their friend's chatter.

"Did your check clear?" Keenan asked Terrance. The cowboys had just done a photo shoot for a hat company, and everyone except for Keenan had gotten paid. It wasn't his first time having issues with his bank.

"My shit didn't clear again," Keenan said, answering his own question.

"It bounced?" Terrance asked. "What happened?"

"'Cause I'm black and I'm young and my hat's real low," Keenan said, laughing, reciting a famous Jay-Z rap line. Terrance laughed so hard, he choked on smoke from the 'wood.

"Chase Bank emailed me saying that the check had an irregular signature, but we called Chase and they said the money cleared and would be put a hold until the twenty-sixth. This shit always happens to me. I need a new phone and I need to pay my rent."

When the basketball games stopped during their youth, some cowboys took up dirt bike riding, which became as popular as riding horses at one point on the farms. It was a phase for some, but not for Anthony and Terrance, who continued to ride bikes as adults in local groups on the weekends.

The music continued to play and the group continued to celebrate Anthony and T-man's birthdays. They were the eldest of the group and had acted like mentors to a lot of the guys over the years. When disagreements occurred, they were usually the first ones to settle them. Both of them had been members of the Acacia Blocc Crips, but at this point in their life they weren't actively gang-banging, though they were still very much connected to the streets.

"Help me with these cans, y'all," Anthony said, getting up to load the back of his truck with recycled bottles and cans that he had been collecting for months. The sound of bottles rattled as he counted how much money he was going to make from this batch.

"That's ten, twenty, twenty-five, forty, sixty, eighty," he said, reciting the numbers. "Shit, I may make me close to a hundred dollars on this run!"

"You better do the speed limit, nigga," Terrance said. "'Cause if you don't, the bums are gonna be happy if they spill out into the street, and if they find them, they'll definitely make it rain." He gestured a brushing motion over his right hand.

"That's at least a couple hundred right there," Rasheed interjected in his deep baritone voice, looking through a pair of dark sunglasses at the collection of bottles in the back of his truck. "You got bottles, plastic, and glass. All the good shit, mayne."

"I tried to teach y'all the game," Anthony said, smiling. "But y'all don't listen to me!"

Keenan and Rasheed started roughhousing each other nearby. "You better back up, you big-bad-wolf-ass-looking nigga," Keenan told Rasheed while puffing his chest out in the air. "I'm not a little nigga no more."

"Oh, that's what you on?" Rasheed asked, holding a puff of smoke in his mouth.

Layton was back from the liquor store with two bottles of Jameson for Anthony and Terrance. "Happy birthday, my niggas," he said while passing them the bottles.

"Thanks, cuz," Terrance responded, reaching into his back pocket for a jar full of different types of weed strands. "This that wax and weed, it's mixed," he said, holding on to the jar. "These the moon rocks that I sprinkle these pine cones of the weed with. When that shit breaks off it's called the keef—it's weed, then keef on the outside, then the moon rocks. It really fucks you up."

Byron sat on a chair removed from the group. He listened to the conversations that the cowboys were having and reflected on his own bouts with drug addiction. The scene reminded him of the days and nights that he had spent with his own friends throughout Compton. The days when he didn't sell any CDs and was forced to steal from his own family to support his drug habit. Those days were long gone, but the memories were crystal clear in each cowboy.

TWO DAYS HAD passed since Anthony and Terrance's birthday, and Randy decided to call a group meeting on a Sunday afternoon to discuss some issues that had been affecting the group. Everyone gathered around and sat on the bleachers in two rows, Charles, Layton, Keiara, and Terrance next to one another and the rest of the group on nearby chairs. Only Randy and Kenneth sat away from the group. Their distance spoke to the rift that Kenneth's alcoholism had created.

Kenneth's behavior was drawing increasing dissent between the cowboys. Every time he drank he transformed into a different person. He picked fights with people and turned into his alter ego, Stona-man, a persona that he had created in recent years. Some wanted him completely out of the group, while others wanted to fight him for the things he would say while intoxicated. He was beginning to lose control and everyone in the group sensed it.

The energy of the meeting was solemn and every word that came out of Randy's mouth felt calculated. It was a much different atmosphere than the birthday celebrations that had taken place only days before.

Meetings tended to be called when Randy felt the need to address certain issues. Part of the increasing trouble that he was facing was that he needed help running the cowboys and the ranch. The pressure was mounting, and with big plans for the future, including the renaming of the Junior Posse as the Compton Junior Equestrian, and the rollout of a ranch renovation project, it was time for him to acknowledge what many in the group had already sensed: he couldn't run the ranch on his own anymore. He needed help.

Part of running the cowboys was establishing a code of conduct for everyone to follow. Like the gangs that operated around the ranch, the cowboys also operated on a strict code of respect and loyalty. Fights and internal conflict were mounting within the group and affecting the dynamics of the cowboys' relationships, and according to Randy, they "needed to be out," he said during the meeting.

It was the second meeting of the year and Randy wanted to establish the plans for the upcoming youth program. Each cowboy would have to make time in their schedule to give back to the program, even if it meant less time for their own rides around the neighborhood. Keiara, a twenty-nine-year-old, and the only woman in the group, and Anthony also had questions about upcoming photo shoots. Money was scarce for everyone, and some wondered how the selection process for shoots took place.

"Why wasn't I selected for that shoot?" Keiara sternly asked while holding her daughter Taylor in her arms. "What's your process like for picking who gets to do what?"

All eyes were on Randy while he took a moment to think about how to respond. The young leader was entrusted with the entire Compton Cowboys operation, and even though many of the cowboys were older than he was, they trusted him with a big part of their livelihood. Whenever a local company reached out to the cowboys to hire them for photo shoots, he was in charge of delegating who would get selected. He was the mastermind behind the entire operation, and lately, Kenneth tended to be chosen over everybody else, which raised questions among the group.

"It's a process that I have no control over," Randy said. "The people who contact me have an idea for who they want to see, and I don't have any control over who gets picked. I wish I had more say, but I don't."

Everyone on the benches listened intently to what Randy had to say and nodded their heads. "Oh, okay, I see," Keiara said while Taylor squirmed in her arms.

Toward the end of the meeting, Randy finally brought up the topic that everyone at the meeting had been waiting to hear about. "The ranch will continue to run after Mayisha retires," he said as everyone's eyes widened with anticipation. "Anthony and Carlton will still have jobs, and there's nothing really to worry about. Everything will be fine. You have to trust me."

The news quelled some of Anthony's fears about the future, but it still didn't prevent him from thinking about other jobs should the ranch close down. He thought about the side hustle mechanic business that he had in the projects; maybe that could sustain him for a few months if the ranch did close.

At the end of the day, the only thing, Randy believed, that could stop them would be themselves.

"With that said, we have to do a better job at protecting the ranch," he explained while continuing to look into everyone's eyes. His voice softened and he was on the verge of tears. "This is a real ranch and a real situation back here, so when we bring people here they have to feel what we feel. They have to feel peace, love, and harmony. Let's do a better job of handling our drama and all the behind-the-scenes bullshit." He paused for a moment, scanning the group. He knew Mayisha's fears about the fate of the ranch. Money problems aside, the recent behavior of some of the guys—smoking, drinking, fighting—was putting the whole operation in jeopardy. "We have to look in the mirror and ask how we each can contribute to the group and make the group better."

SKITTLES

RANDY HAD A POINT. THE ranch was a place filled with love and peace and harmony. That was something Anthony felt in his heart while he toiled there at 5 a.m. every morning. The urgency of preserving the ranch was starting to kick in and his own history with it and the horses came into clear focus.

Long before Anthony learned to put a saddle on a horse, before he learned how to keep a Stetson hat crisp by brushing it counterclockwise, he was a gangster.

Anthony's initiation into the Acacia Blocc gang occurred in the early hours of a humid late spring morning on Acacia Avenue in 1991. He was eight years old. His mother had recently walked out, leaving his father to raise him single-handedly, a task that was nearly impossible for Thaddeus Harris, who worked as a high school janitor on the other side of town and couldn't be home to supervise or keep Anthony out of reach of the local gang.

Anthony was alone in his house when three hard knocks interrupted his breakfast and the voice of his older friend, Tre, boomed outside the double-bolted door.

"Come outside, Anthony!" Tre, a neighborhood elder, said. "Don't take all day."

He had spent the entire night thinking about this moment, knowing they could come for him at any time. He pushed his bowl of cornflakes aside and approached the door, rested his hand on the deadbolt and peered out through the peephole.

Five people stood at the bottom of his front stoop. Tre, Marcus, and a few other kids from the neighborhood. They were between the ages of twelve and twenty-five, and each wore a blue handkerchief on their shoulder, a badge of honor that indicated they'd been inducted into the Acacia Blocc Crips themselves. Like Anthony, they had all come from broken homes, but now they were fixed up as the youngest recruits who would be raised within the hierarchy of one of the most notorious gangs in Compton, feared by their enemies and by local law enforcement. Drug dealing, extortion, and murder were central to the Acacia Blocc operation.

Outside, Tre continued to yell loud enough for the neighbors to hear. "Come on out! We know you're home."

Anthony unlocked the first bolt, then the second, and then took a deep breath.

He thought about his family. Not the family of the dysfunctional home he was born into. Not the relatives his father had spoken about for years in his home state of Louisiana, or his mother's family, local Compton residents who had also journeyed from the Deep South. The family that crossed his mind were the very people who would in a few minutes violently pound his eight-year-old body into the pavement in front of all of his neighbors.

The violence was justified, he felt. Getting jumped into the set was about proving your loyalty and earning respect. After this fight, he would have a family he could go to for anything, both big and small, and they would always have his back. It would make up for the absence of love and attention he felt at home.

In the city of Compton, these experiences were rites of passage, an intergenerational practice that began with Anthony's uncles and naturally carried over to him. If you lived on or around the Acacia Blocc you were either a part of the gang or you were against them. There was no middle ground. Those who refused to join would be tormented and harassed on a daily basis. They were considered traitors and were often the victims of violent assaults. The only people who received a pass were star athletes who showed promise on the field or on the court, and Anthony, unfortunately, could never dribble a ball or run routes on the football field. But he also wasn't a traitor.

Perhaps subconsciously, even then, a part of him recognized that he was born into a time and place shaped by forces outside his control. That he never really had a choice. That he would always—one day—become a gangster.

Outside, Tre wanted to know if Anthony was ready. He was one of the older cats in the 'hood and someone Anthony looked to for the help his father could not provide. Anthony had shown promise, and Tre finally felt like he was ready.

Anthony opened the door and stepped forward, ready to face the inevitable.

The fight that branded Anthony with the new nickname "Ant Dogg" only lasted five minutes, but it set Anthony on a treacherous path for the next fifteen years.

Soon after the fight, when the bruises on his face and body healed, Anthony received his first gun from one of the gang's elders, a .380-caliber revolver. He kept it on his body at all times. He carried it on his walks to the corner store to buy soda and chips; he carried it to school on the days he decided to go. He and his gun were inseparable, particularly when the Mexican CV 70's began a war with Acacia over drug territories. He even carried his gun to Martin Luther King Jr. Hospital whenever he accompanied his grandmother for her checkups.

But he didn't fire it until two years later, when he was ten years old. The older gang members told him he needed to earn his stripes and forced him to come along on a drive-by shooting on a block controlled by the Tree Top Pirus, a local Blood gang.

Anthony missed his target that night, but the gun made him feel invincible. It gave him a sense of power that he never knew he could have.

The days came and went. Another test, another duty. A shooting, a drug run, a jumping. It wasn't long before Anthony was earning a name for himself on the streets.

It was shortly after he dropped out of middle school that Black told him about a woman he wanted him to meet. Her name was Mayisha and she was teaching the kids in the neighborhood how to ride horses. Anthony had never been to the ranch before, but he was intrigued by rumors of horses and cowboys, of all places, right here in his city, his 'hood.

His father's stories of his early childhood in Louisiana conjured up images of the backcountry roads, the grazing cows, the rustic barns built on rolling green hills. Black had a feeling that Anthony would take a liking to riding, and he was right. Anthony was still a kid, after all, and despite the tough front he had to put up, he'd always been enthralled by the cowboys and horses he'd seen in western movies.

Anthony and Black set off for Richland Farms on a blazingly hot afternoon in August. When they arrived, they were hit by the pungent smell of hay and manure, and the whimsical and frequent neighs of the horses. Anthony had entered a world he never imagined, a world that he thought only existed on the lots of Hollywood studios. He couldn't believe what he was seeing. But this world was real.

They watched a group of horses trot before a row of swaying palm trees and, in the distance, the Compton City Hall building.

It was captivating, like an oasis in the middle of their city. It felt like a place he could call home.

Black pointed to a large sign above the entry to the stables. In bold text it read "Compton Junior Posse: Equestrian Club, Est. 1988" and showed a gold painting of a horse rearing, as if it meant to throw off its rider. Anthony had never seen that word before, "equestrian," but a *posse* was like a gang, wasn't it? If so, he thought, then what did that make a cowboy?

He didn't have much time to figure it out, because a woman was already walking toward them. She was wearing a cowboy hat with a blue stripe wrapping its brim. Clutched under her arm was a dusty leather saddle. She had kind, sparkling eyes, and a purposeful stride as she approached.

"You must be Anthony," she said, extending her free hand.

And that was how he met Mayisha Akbar and the Compton Junior Posse.

Anthony was immediately drawn to the horses. He had never seen anything like them before, and up until that point the only cowboys he had ever seen were white. He quickly met other members of the Posse, kids his own age with names like Rasheed, Terrance, and Koffer. When the school bell rang, he would rush to the ranch with excitement, eager to jump on the back of a horse.

However, he was leading a double life. The time he spent on the ranch allowed him to unplug from the realities of Compton street life. The police helicopters that, he assumed, were chasing friends of his continued to buzz over the ranch, but while he fed the horses and cleaned their stalls, he was free. It felt like they were surveilling him, but he knew he was safe.

Being on the ranch opened him up to feelings of tranquility. When he was on a horse he was exempt from the life of crime and violence that he was living on Acacia Avenue. But even these moments had a daily expiration date on them. As soon as he closed the gate behind him and stepped back onto Caldwell Street, he transformed back into Lil' Ant, one of the youngest and most ambitious members of the Acacia Crips.

"Alright, cuz!" he would yell to anyone he would see before leaving the property and heading home on his bicycle. "I'll see you on the other side!"

As a child, Anthony had always been attracted to flashy cars. He admired the way the older guys on his block drove down the street in their blue chrome Buick Regals and Chevy Impalas as the cars rattled from the powerful kick of the eighteen-inch Alpine speakers in their trunks. Anthony's love for cars also came from the time his father owned a mechanic shop on the westside of Compton. It was there that he learned everything from installing a speaker system to an oil change to installing a new carburetor.

His first car was a Nissan Altima that he bought from a friend for three hundred dollars. But it didn't live up to the thrill he felt when he saw a Buick Regal for the first time. That was love at first sight, and he would stop at nothing to one day own one.

Anthony was faced with a choice: save up for a car the traditional way working for his father, or make money quicker by hustling drugs on his block. He chose the latter.

His first drug deal occurred on the corner of Acacia and Alondra Boulevard when he sold a ten-dollar bag of weed to a local homeless man. His business immediately picked up and within months he had a consistent clientele.

Having money in his pocket felt good. It came quick, and every deal that he made brought an immediate adrenaline rush. As his business prospered, the need to be in school every day began to dwindle. After getting kicked out of Compton High for fighting, he was sent to Inglewood High School, where he was also expelled for fighting. He ended up in a continuation high school, the last resort for at-risk teenagers.

While this was happening, Anthony also began to spend less time at the ranch. He had gotten a taste of drug dealing and wanted more. Above all, he still wanted to buy the car of his dreams. He did what any young hustler in the 'hood would do, moved on from weed to selling more dangerous drugs.

The coop was one of the best-known crack houses on the farms, and it's where Anthony began to spend most of his days. It was an ideal location, just close enough to Wilmington Avenue but also quiet enough not to raise any suspicion. It was once a home but had been repossessed during the early 1990s when the family who lived there were unable to continue payments on their home. The backyard once had a thriving chicken coop, but the first time Anthony set foot on the property it held only the remains of wilted feathers and dried feces. Every door except for the back was bolted shut as a safety measure for both the inhabitants and the dealers who lived there. Every fiend who walked to the front door was received either by Anthony or by one of his trusted associates.

"What do you want?" he would yell from the other side of the door while as many as fifteen people smoked crack cocaine on the living room floor behind him. Sometimes the drug fiends would stay for as long as two weeks, finding creative ways to support their addiction by completing tasks around the home like cleaning or delivering food for Anthony and his friends. Sometimes, when the fiends would get out of hand, Anthony would be forced to respond with the threat of his gun or physical violence.

The money he earned at the coop helped Anthony purchase

his dream car, a 1992 Buick Regal with one of the best hydraulic systems on his block. At seventeen years old, he was riding in style. His Regal came with a shiny navy blue paint job, the same color of the bandana he wore on his forehead.

Earning money stoked his appetite for more. While he earned upwards of five thousand dollars a day, he also supplemented his income by stealing cars. Sometimes he would get caught, sometimes he wouldn't. On days when business was slow at the coop, he and his friends would go looking for Mexican men to rob. The Mexicans wore expensive ostrich boots and flashy belt buckles on Friday and Saturday nights. Those boots alone would bring in at least two hundred dollars, and if they were lucky, there would be more money stashed inside them.

Anthony was eighteen the first time he went to jail for grand theft auto. He had been caught a few months before he turned eighteen but released the same day because he was a minor. Being eighteen, however, came with a different reality. This time he was locked up for three weeks. A year later he was jailed again for possession of a firearm. A year after that he would be caught again.

The first and last time the police would ever bust into Anthony's home was on an early August morning.

"Fuck," Anthony said when he heard the door violently crash open. "They're here for me."

As his home filled up with more than ten police officers, he immediately thought about the movie scenes he had watched as a kid, films like *Scarface* and *Goodfellas*. Getting busted, as each of these films depicted, was almost like a rite of passage. It was a way to earn stripes and respect, and when the officers burst into his room, he didn't put up a fight. Instead he calmly put his hands in the air. He had known this day would eventually come.

As one officer handcuffed him and read him his rights over the barking of police dogs, another group of officers reached under his bed and grabbed his hidden backpacks full of cocaine. A different group cut open his living room sofa and found other packages of cocaine. They had found his stash. But all Anthony could think about was the tens of thousands of dollars in cash that he had buried in his backyard. It was enough, he hoped, to eventually bail him out.

The judge didn't offer Anthony the bail he expected, and his public defender—or "public pretender," as they were known in the 'hood—did the very least for him. He suggested Anthony take a two-year plea deal, which is exactly what he did. Within a few weeks he was off to a federal prison in California near the Mexican border.

As a member of the Acacia Crips, Anthony was relegated to a side of the prison for black inmates. Latinos, whites, and everyone else were lumped into separate holding cells because of the frequent race riots. As Anthony settled into a cell with a black man from Northern California, he began to think about what his friends and family were doing back in Compton. Being locked up meant that he would be forced to cope with true isolation. While he sometimes ran into friends that he knew from Compton, life in prison meant that he would be completely removed from the horses he dreamt about on Mayisha's ranch.

The first three weeks were the hardest. Prison was unlike the time he had served in Los Angeles County jails. This was an entirely different world, and he was forced to become tougher and more hardened the minute he arrived. He had to fight to let his fellow inmates know that he wasn't a punk, and had to fight to let people know that he wasn't afraid of them. He had to man up quickly and find smart ways to survive within the prison walls. He did push-ups daily and fought other prisoners, often just to prove a point—that he wasn't afraid of them. If he didn't, it showed weakness, and that meant more difficult times ahead.

He got into a total of ten fights during his first three weeks, both with old enemies from back in Los Angeles and with other inmates who were intent on testing him. Anthony got into so many fights that he got sent to "the hole" and sat in a room that was more isolating than his eight-by-six-foot cell. The hole was a dark, small, one-person cell meant to isolate testy inmates from the rest of the prison population. If the correctional officers believed you were in any way involved in a fight, you were sent there. The goal was to deter future transgressions, but the hole was also a way to psychologically break inmates down. It was a place where the screams and wails of grown men could be heard at night, echoing throughout the prison.

Anthony spent a total of two weeks in the hole's darkness. The only light that came into the room was through a small rectangular opening through which he received food three times a day. The darkness made it hard to see what he was eating. Mealtime was the only time when he would hear another human voice, even if it belonged to a white man who hated everything that the color of Anthony's skin represented.

"It's time to eat, Harris," the officer would yell, opening the window, depositing the food, then slamming it shut.

The first year was the hardest. During his free time, Anthony spent hours exercising in the prison yard or running laps around the makeshift track that some of the inmates had created. He was never an athlete, but having a chiseled body and staying in peak shape wasn't about impressing girls anymore; in prison it became a matter of survival. The stronger he got the better he could defend himself.

Because he was a newcomer, he continued to make a name for himself by proving his toughness to the rest of the prison population. Inmates were housed in different cells and sections of the prison according to their race. African-Americans and Latinos, who comprised the majority of the prison population, had the largest sections and were housed on opposite sides of the prison. Race riots were common, and every section in prison was run like a complex organization, a Fortune 500 company, even. Resources and money were allocated for different reasons according to one's needs. There was a formal code, and then there was the code that Anthony was forced to live by. Some weeks were better than others. But Anthony wouldn't have to fight only his own battles in prison. He was often asked to fight and discipline fellow inmates who didn't obey the rules.

As Anthony's first year began to round out, he found himself spending less and less time on the prison yard and more time in the solitude of his own cell. Though it had been years since he last rode a horse, in isolation his mind kept returning to the horses he used to ride at Mayisha's ranch. Minutes turned into hours and hours turned into days as he dreamed about the feeling of riding bareback through the streets of Compton. He missed the feeling of working on the ranch and riding around the Richland Farms on Misty, the horse his father had purchased for him when he was eleven. When his cell gates opened up twice a day for recreation, he opted out and stayed inside and did push-ups in his cell. He was slowly withdrawing from prison life and an environment meant to control him.

One day, he felt compelled to draw and paint, though he'd never done so before. He began to draw images of wild horses and aspects of the ranch that were vivid in his memory. He drew the contours of the giant oak tree that housed hundreds of chirping birds every morning. He drew groups of black boys and girls, as he remembered them, riding on horses wearing light blue T-shirts, like the ones Mayisha required everyone to wear on the ranch. Drawing materials were scarce, but Anthony managed to trade batteries with other inmates for a notepad and pencils.

The first time he drew horses, they looked nothing like horses. The figures were weirdly shaped brown blotches that barely resembled an animal. But just like riding, practice made perfect, and after several months Anthony's drawings morphed into realistic illustrations.

He began checking out books from the prison library that had horses in them. He checked out children's books, history books, and animal books, anything that had images of horses that could serve as a model to improve his drawing. He spent hours sketching them onto another sheet of paper and putting them up in his cell, creating a makeshift art gallery for passersby to admire.

Inmates weren't allowed to have colored pencils or paint because correctional officers feared they could be used to make makeshift narcotics that could be sniffed or ingested, but Anthony worked with what he had and devised a method for creating watercolor paintings in his cell using Skittles candy, a favorite among inmates and highly sought after. If the candy's colored dye could leave a mark on his fingers, he thought, then it would be sure to also leave a mark on a sheet of paper. He was right. He dipped individual candies into a bowl of water one afternoon and shouted with excitement, almost loud enough for the guards to burst in and shut his secret operation down.

Anthony learned by experimentation that if he wanted to paint a brown horse, he should mix red, blue, and yellow together. If he wanted a black horse, he should mix red and green Skittles. His drawings became lifelike with the color that the Skittles provided, giving them a texture that he could feel. He painted every day, sometimes long into the early hours of the morning while his cell-mate groaned in the top bunk and Anthony crouched near the bars, painting under a dull, flickering light outside of his cell.

In a matter of months, other inmates started calling him the "painter" and requested their own horse drawings.

The watercolor paintings that he painted every day were meant to keep him out of trouble. But they did more than that. They kept him alive. Drawing and painting horses for hours at a time helped him cope with the realities of being locked up in a cell meant to eradicate every ounce of humanity from his body. Painting horses reminded him of the world that existed outside of the eight-by-six cement walls and the humanity that every stroke of paint brought him closer to having again.

Every week on the phone, he spoke with Lozita, his girlfriend and mother of his two children, and told her about his plans to ride horses and work on the ranch once he got out. She supported him and continued to send money to fill up his prison commissary so he could buy more materials for his paintings. During one call, he told her that if he had never stopped riding horses, he would never have gone to jail. She agreed.

As he painted more and more horses, he made a decision that this would be the last time he would ever spend in prison. His daughter, Acacia, was five years old, and his son, Anthony Jr., was two. He wanted to be around for them and knew that getting back to the horses in the Richland Farms would be the only way to do that.

TWO WEEKS AFTER Anthony was released from his two-year sentence, he decided it was time to go back and visit the ranch. He felt the same nervousness that he had felt the first time Black brought him there so many years ago. It had been more than ten years and nothing had changed, he thought to himself. The blue-and-white-painted Compton Junior Posse sign still hung high over the ranch's entrance, but now it was weathered from storms and in need of a fresh coat of paint. The storage shed that housed the hay, tools, and general equipment still looked like it was in need of a proper cleanup. There was more dirt in the arena and a few new horses, but practically everything else remained the same.

Most importantly, he felt the same peace that he had felt as a child.

Anthony immediately spotted Mayisha sitting on the bleachers with a group of youth riders. Some were faces he recognized from the community, while others were new.

"Is that who I think it is?" Mayisha excitedly yelled as Anthony walked up to the group wearing a pair of dark blue jeans, an extra-large white T-shirt, and black Nike sneakers.

"You know it," replied Anthony as he approached Mayisha for a hug he had been dreaming about for the past two years.

As the hug with Mayisha came to a close, Anthony looked at the tightly coiled dreadlocks that had greyed since he last saw her. Her soft blue-hazel eyes hadn't changed. Neither had her cinnamon-brown skin.

She looked at Anthony like a mother who hadn't seen her own child in years. As if her own son had just gotten out of prison for the same crimes she had fought so hard to keep her riders from committing.

Still, Anthony, like all the other riders who had been part of her program, would always be family.

"Welcome back, Anthony," Mayisha said as she continued to

hold him for what seemed like an eternity. It had been two and a half years since the last time they had held one another. The warmth of her hug took him back to the memories of their camping trips and trail rides that she had organized for kids from the Compton Junior Posse. Those trips, he remembered, were the only times he had ever left Compton.

She grabbed his arms and then his shoulders and then looked at him with a pair of seasoned eyes that had seen hundreds of boys and girls grow up from children to adults. The dark brown eyes that looked back at her were the same ones that she had seen grow up, but something about them looked different. The eyes that she stared at had seen things in prison that no human should ever be forced to see: murder, rape, violence, and terror.

Anthony wondered if it would be the right time to ask Mayisha if he could come back to work on the ranch as a groundskeeper. After all, this was the plan he and Lozita had discussed during their weekly phone calls over the past year. He figured that working on the ranch would be the only way to keep himself from going back to prison for a parole violation. He hadn't been an active member of the ranch since he was fifteen, and a lot had changed since then. He was an ex-convict and had very few options to find legal work. Most well-paying jobs required a high school diploma and would not accept an ex-felon regardless of their rehabilitation. The odds and the system were completely stacked against him and he was faced with two options: go back to hustling on the streets or turn his life around by recommitting to horses and working on the ranch. His future rested in Mayisha's hands.

Anthony didn't muster the courage to ask her about working for her that day. There were too many people around and it would be another two weeks before he would eventually bring up the subject.

"You want to come back and work on the ranch?" Mayisha inquisitively asked two weeks later. They were sitting on a bench overlooking the arena. Anthony nodded his head, a bottle of Sprite in his hands.

"You know we don't have a lot of positions open right now, right?"

"Yeah, Mayisha," Anthony quickly replied. "I came to ask for a chance to work on the ranch. My parole officer said I have to find a job, and you know it's hard for people to find work once they get out of prison. If I don't find something, I'll go right back to the streets. Probably back to prison."

Mayisha looked out at the horses. "Maybe we can figure something out for you," she said. "There's already somebody working as the groundskeeper, but they'll be leaving soon. Come back next week and we'll figure something out."

Anthony was overjoyed. Drawing horses had kept him alive in prison, and caring for them would also help him stay alive back in the city of Compton. The old Anthony would have moved back to the Acacia Blocc to be with his friends, but he knew if he wanted to stay out of trouble he had to live somewhere else.

Within a week he had moved into the Imperial Courts housing projects with Lozita and their children. His new two-bedroom apartment was humble but big enough for his family. Unlike his prison cell, his room had a door that he could open and close when he pleased, and a light switch that he could turn on and off.

The first few weeks were the toughest. Sometimes when he woke up in the morning, he would look around and pause, expecting to hear the barking orders from correctional officers who controlled every second of his life. It both relieved and scared him to know that the old order was gone, but the structure of prison had become so ingrained in him that his body felt lost without it. When he couldn't sleep, he found himself getting up in the middle of the night to check on his children who slept in the next room.

The phone didn't stop ringing, but every time someone from his past called and asked for him, he would tell his daughter or his wife to say that he wasn't home. He knew his old crew would be getting in touch, and that meant trouble.

On top of his having to hide from his old friends, Anthony's new neighborhood also provided its own unique challenges. The "blue bricks," as the Imperial Courts projects were called, were home to the PJ Watts Crips, and to the Grape Street Crips, who were located in a nearby housing project. Both of these gangs at one point had been at war with the Acacia Crips. As it stood, Anthony would be in danger, especially with a conspicuous "A" tattoo on the left side of his neck, which everyone in Compton and Watts knew meant that he was from the Acacia Crips.

To Anthony's surprise, nothing happened the first week after he moved into his new neighborhood. He introduced himself to members of the PJ Watts Crips and assured them that he had left that life behind.

"I'm an old head," he described to the young men in the projects. "I done paid my dues already and lived that life."

After a few weeks, head nods turned into handshakes and then into hugs. People started calling him "O.G. Ant"—short for "original gangster"—as a form of respect. In the meantime, Anthony and his family were busy catching up on the birthdays, football games, and holiday parties that they had missed while he was locked up.

Anthony's workday on the ranch usually began at 5 a.m. and ended around 12 p.m. His schedule allowed him to pick up his children from school every day and be present in their lives in ways that he only dreamed of when he was imprisoned. He never had been an early riser, but he grew accustomed to the 5 a.m. early morning wake-up calls in prison. Being on the ranch before anyone arrived gave him a feeling of peace that he had yearned for for so many years. The early mornings were still and quiet and mysterious.

The more removed he became from the life he used to live, the closer he became with the horses on the ranch. Dakota, a ten-year-old short-haired black American quarter horse, became his best friend. He began to confide in her while brushing and braiding her hair every morning. He told Dakota things that he couldn't say to anyone else and shared some of the horrors that he had witnessed in prison. When he spoke to her his voice transformed into a soft, caring version of himself. Parts of the boy who had left when he first got jumped into the Acacia Crips returned during these conversations. Dakota listened. He spoke. It became a cycle that was repeated every single morning. He could be soft and tender and share anything with her, which fought off the message that the world had forced on him—that black men couldn't be soft.

The biggest thrill was the moment he freed Dakota from her stall and let her run into the arena. It was a feeling he knew too well. He related to her, knew what she felt. Freeing her from her stall every morning became the highlight of his day, as if he were atoning for all the days he was locked up. He knew what it felt like to be caged for hours at a time. Her stall was the same size as the cell that he used to spend his entire day in. His was surrounded by cement walls, hers by long metal gates, and both were controlled by someone who decided whether or not they could leave. The resemblance was uncanny.

When Anthony rode his bike to the ranch every morning, he could hear Dakota neighing, waiting for him to open the gate so that she could jump and run around the arena and play in the dirt.

"I'm on my way, girl!" he would say as he walked to the back of the ranch.

Her joy meant everything to Anthony. The time he spent in prison had made it hard for him to express his feelings and fears. But he did not feel that around Dakota.

After a while, Lozita also began to see this change. Anthony was opening up to her and his family in ways that seemed impossible before. He started calling his father more often. He smiled more and spent more time around the home. When he picked up his children from school every day he hugged and kissed them and told them how much he cared for them, how much he loved them. If they behaved well, he would ride to their school and pick them up on Dakota. This was also the point in his life when he attempted to reconcile with his mother, who had abandoned him and his father. Forgiving her for leaving him as a child was one of the toughest things he had to do. He did it with the help of Dakota.

On the ranch Anthony became one of the most sought-out mentors. Children gravitated toward him because of his knowledge of horses and his willingness to help them become better riders.

"You guys know what the rules of the ranch are, right?" he would ask eager groups of children between the ages of eight and fifteen the same way Mayisha had taught him years before. "Rule number one is you have to clean up the stables before you can ride the horses. Rule number two is you have to feed the horses, brush their coats, and clean their hooves. After that, and only after that, you can ride."

KEIARA'S SONG (HER PAIN)

KEIARA NEEDED TO CLEAR HER mind after Randy's meeting, so she drove to the stable in nearby Gardena with Taylor. Though she typically felt more comfortable around men than women, being the only woman in the group was becoming a challenge, especially when she and Randy didn't always see eye to eye. When rides or events were planned, no other cowboy had to worry about childcare. Even those who had children usually relied on their wives or girlfriends. That freedom was a luxury that she didn't have as a single mother with a three-year-old. It was something the other cowboys simply didn't understand.

Taylor fussed and pleaded to ride Penny all by herself. Her round brown eyes were fixed on Keiara like a hawk's.

It's not that her mother minded Taylor's tantrum. She preferred a tantrum over horses to the ones about not wanting to eat her vegetables, and Taylor's unflinching enthusiasm brought her joy. Horse riding had been in their family for three generations and Taylor, she believed, would keep the tradition alive.

"Taylor, stop playing so much and get your leg up in the saddle, girl," Keiara told her one-year-old. They stood in the riding arena as she placed Taylor's tiny body on the dark brown saddle. "Okay, you ready? Mommy is going to hold you, but you're going to be on your own, okay?"

Taylor nodded.

The breeze blew softly around them, gently moving between Keiara and her daughter as she slowly pulled the brown quarter horse Penny around the empty arena. Riding around the arena with her mother was Taylor's favorite pastime. When she wasn't riding horses, Taylor was talking about riding horses. Her day-care teachers kept a tally of how many times during the day she spoke about horses; it was always a double-digit number.

Taylor was a regular at the stables, and fellow riders all took a liking to the little girl whose brown eyes gleamed with joy around any horse she could get her hands on, big or small.

Being surrounded by horses was a family tradition for the pair, with their deep roots in rural Mississippi. Horses were a fixture on both sides of Keiara's family for as far back as anyone could remember. Keiara's maternal grandmother, Mimi, got a horse as a gift from her husband, Spurgeon McClendon, also known around Compton as Joe Bleed, and also introduced Keiara's mother, Jennifer, to competitive horse riding, which she did until Keiara was a teenager.

Keiara walked the horse around the arena for about twenty minutes before Taylor started to get antsy. The glaring afternoon sun beat down, and her two pigtails bounced from side to side while Penny trotted slowly. After a few laps, Taylor's uneasiness picked up, and within moments she searched for her mother's eyes again.

"Mommy," she softly whispered. "Mommy."

Keiara knew what was coming next. This was usually when Taylor's soft whimper would transform into a full cry, meaning it was time to go to the bathroom. Or, worse, it meant that she had already soiled her diaper.

This time, however, the timing of Taylor's bathroom break fortuitously coincided with the fact that Keiara also needed to give herself a rest. Just a few days before, a sudden movement had triggered a sensation in her lower back that swelled with a piercing pain that shot down through her entire lower torso. She rubbed the lower part of her back, right above her waist.

After a car accident the year before, her back had required months of rehabilitation and rest. It was her first major injury as an adult and the most painful because it forced her to take almost a year off from competing in the rodeo circuit. Not being able to ride and compete in the barrel races was one of the hardest things she had ever had to endure. Riding was all she had ever known. Even after giving birth to Taylor, she was back on the circuit in a matter of months. Nothing would keep her from saddling up.

Keiara's entire identity had revolved around horses for as long as she could remember. They were central to who she was, and, like Taylor, she had begun riding when she was a toddler, eventually working up to competing in the Bill Pickett Invitational Rodeo, one of the only black rodeos in the United States, at the age of ten.

Getting healthy again was the number one priority for Keiara. Her dream of becoming the first black woman to compete in the national rodeo championships was no small feat given her work schedule and her duties as a mother. Accomplishing her dream required a full commitment and a rigorous training schedule, which she frequently balanced with the pressures of being a single mother.

On days that she didn't have to work, her mornings usually consisted of either a gym workout session or a visit to the physical therapist, who would perform hours of therapy on her back and her shoulder. Sometimes the sessions were painful, but it was the lesser of two evils: she preferred that pain over the agony of not being able to ride at all. On days when her daughter didn't have to go to daycare, she brought her to the stables. Though she loved bringing Taylor along, being alone with her horse in the arena brought her the most joy. It reminded her of her first horse, a brown Thoroughbred named Skip that she bought with her own money at the age of fifteen.

Like other children who grew up in Compton during the 1990s, Keiara had lived in a world that was almost entirely consumed by gangs and violence. The violence usually occurred outside her home, but sometimes it also seeped inside of it. The home that she grew up in was divided into a front and a back house. Keiara stayed with her grandparents and siblings in the front, while her mother lived in the back, away from the family, following years of disagreements. Her Mississippi-born grandfather, the head of the family, was a stern man and the first person in his family to migrate out west during the height of the Great Migration. He was subsequently followed by his siblings, aunts, and other relatives. He was the only father figure she ever knew; her biological father, who was serving a twenty-year sentence in a federal prison in Minnesota, was incarcerated when she was two years old and released when she was eighteen.

Like other black men who grew up in that era, her grandfather took to alcohol to numb his isolation and frustration at the lack of opportunities that he had expected to find in California. The West Coast dream—that of endless employment and a place free of the entrenched racism of the South—never quite reached fruition for him. He found California to have its own system of racial inequality, often more challenging to confront than the blatant abuses of Jim Crow. So Keiara's grandfather found refuge in the bottle, which allowed him to temporarily escape the realities that he was forced to reckon with. It also created deep tension in his home and verbal abuse toward his family.

Still, the violence inside Keiara's home was eclipsed by what she experienced outside of it. Bullets often flew from various directions in her community. Sometimes they flew out of the guns of black men who wore blue, sometimes out of the guns of black men who wore red. Sometimes they flew out of the guns of people who wore black and white.

Though she was never in a gang, Keiara was always gang-affiliated; her friends and relatives were in the local neighborhood gang. Even if she had tried, there was no way to fully escape the wrath of the 135 Bloods or the Westside Pirus. Growing up next to the horse stables near the border of South Central and Compton called the Hill helped her escape the violence. She received a pass from the Pirus when she rode her horse around her neighborhood and became the "girl who rode horses" at school. Outside of class she was teased, but it never fazed her. It only motivated her to ride more often and continue to develop a language of silent compassion with the horses.

At thirteen Keiara began competing in rodeos throughout the state. Her mother and her mother's friend would often be the only black people in attendance. She could remember being one of the only black people out of five hundred competitors. Nobody spoke to her until she started winning money. It was just her and her little black horse out there getting it.

With success, the trajectory of Keiara's life became clearer. White competitors didn't want to see a black girl from Compton take all of the winnings. It was her introduction to discrimination, to people who thought a young black girl from the 'hood had no business competing in rodeos. The reactions to her presence at mostly white rodeos made participating in the Bill Pickett Rodeo, a black circuit, feel closer to home. Being around black riders and competitors felt familiar, and she was instantly introduced to black riders from all over the United States, communities where black cowboys and cowgirls weren't the exception, but the norm.

While Keiara competed in weekend rodeo events, an entirely different reality was quickly approaching. The brief stares and the glances she received from young boys and men evolved into longer looks. She was beginning to receive attention from men in ways that she had never experienced before. Her body was developing, and by the age of twelve she was often confused for being much older than she really was.

She developed a crush on her best friend's older brother, a seventeen-year-old known for his good looks and popularity in the neighborhood. She got goose bumps whenever he entered the room and experienced new feelings for him that she feared sharing with her mother and close friends.

One night while she was sleeping over at her best friend's house, she was awakened by the creaking sound of the bedroom door while her friend slept across the room. The door opened slightly, revealing the contours of what appeared to be her crush, his broad shoulders outlined by the light of a moonlit window. He slipped into her bed and began to kiss and touch her body. The feeling was electric and chilling. She didn't make a sound and was paralyzed by a rush of blood that coursed through her body, but also by a growing sense of fear as he whispered into her ear.

"It's okay," he said, pulling his pants down and forcing himself upon her. She couldn't move and knew what was about to happen. He palmed her mouth, his breath hot against her ear. "It's okay, Keiara."

Her friend woke up a few minutes later to see her brother on top of Keiara. She immediately pushed him off of her. "Get out of here!" she yelled while punching his back as he ran out of the room.

The event left a chilling memory that Keiara couldn't shake. But it would not be the last time she would be molested by her friend's brother. It happened again in the same room and in the same home. Her friend didn't stop her brother the second time. She tried to say something but no sound came out, and he continued until he finished and pulled his pants up and walked out of the room.

Both experiences left Keiara deeply confused about her own body. She was immediately forced to accept his message that said her body wasn't hers to own. That her body was up for grabs. She feared telling anyone about the experience because she was sure they'd blame her for it. She felt ashamed, and the silence of the assault left her completely mute.

Keiara stopped believing in her body after that night. It created a sense of agonizing emptiness that remained long after the rape. The only person she spoke to about it was her horse, Skip. Her emptiness crystallized into resentment toward herself and others, and riding her horse became more than a hobby—it became a matter of survival.

She began driving around this time and purchased her own vehicle so she could drive to see her horse every day after school. At home, she continued to hang out with local gangsters. She began dating some of them and often found herself in precarious situations, particularly after getting a "P" tattoo on the back of her neck with a crown and a star, an emblem that represented the Piru neighborhood she was from.

The life Keiara led in school didn't always reflect the one she lived after school got out. She began drinking and driving and smoking weed with friends. But she kept her grades up and was functional to the point where nobody suspected anything. She applied to different colleges and got accepted into Prairie View A&M, a historically black college near Houston, with a rodeo school. It was the only school that would allow her to continue to ride horses while continuing her education. It was a dream come true and brought her closer to realizing her goal of becoming a national barrel racing champion.

Still, leaving Compton was difficult. Compton wasn't easy, but it was the community she had grown up in. But worse was her younger brother, Jerrod.

Jerrod was well into high school by the time Keiara left for college. The two had grown extremely close as children, a relationship that often left Keiara feeling more like his mother than his older sister. She had looked after him since she was ten. In high school, she picked him up from wherever he was and dropped him off at friends' homes, ensuring that he was safe at all times. She even fought other boys in the neighborhood who picked on him because of his slight build. Jerrod meant the world to her.

Right before she left, he began to change, maturing right before her eyes. Though he was always affiliated with the local gangs in their neighborhood, he became fully integrated in the 'hood. He joined the 135 Eastside Piru Blood gang right before she left for Texas the first time.

"If you're going to join the gang," she advised him, "you have to lift weights and get stronger so other people won't overpower you."

While she worried about her brother's safety, being at a historically black college was transformative. She had never been around so many black people who prioritized education and also came from the 'hood. On her first day on campus, she met a young woman who had also attended her high school, and they became close and each other's support system.

But while Keiara was away, she also dealt with the harsh realities of survivor's guilt. She questioned her survival and ability to make it out of the 'hood. She kept thinking about all the people she had left behind in Compton and questioned why she deserved a better life than them, or rather, why she deserved to escape from the violence that trapped them. Reconciling this reality made it hard to be away from her community, particularly as she noticed her brother sliding deeper and deeper into the streets. Their phone calls became less frequent. Her mother called her, worried about Jerrod's safety. "I'm scared for him," she would say, and when Keiara did speak with her brother on the phone, the conversations became superficial. There were things he was going through that they felt he couldn't discuss over the phone. Code words were often used to describe the murders of friends and the money that he was making from selling drugs. The roles had reversed. Jerrod was now the protector of the family and in control of the neighborhood.

EVERYTHING CHANGED DURING the early morning of Sunday, September 28, 2014. The phone rang at 4 a.m. while Keiara was sleeping in her boyfriend's home in Louisiana, where she was visiting him for the weekend.

"Why is Kevin calling me this late?" she asked herself as she looked at the name of her brother's close friend on her phone. "He must be drunk or something."

She ignored the call and fell back asleep. The phone rang again and again.

"Hello?" she said, still half asleep.

"Kiki, Jerrod's gone!" Kevin yelled on the phone while crying hysterically. "He's gone!"

"What do you mean he's gone?" she wearily replied.

Kevin's girlfriend grabbed the phone. "Mimi just called us, and we're on our way over to the hospital now," she said. "Call Mimi. Call Mimi."

After calling Mimi to confirm the news of her brother's death, Keiara broke down in a state of shock. Jerrod had been shot in the head by a member of the Westside Pirus in an apparent setup. They had been looking for him for weeks and the streets had finally caught up with him.

Keiara took a plane home the next day and cried during the entire flight. Coming home from Texas was usually a joyous occasion. A close friend or relative would usually pick her up from the airport. But this time the occasion was different. There was no celebration, only the shattered looks of people who had heard this song play before. Like Jerrod, Keiara's uncle had also died at the age of twenty-three. His death had left an open wound in her family, and now the wound had grown.

It usually took law enforcement weeks or months to find someone's killer. Sometimes it took longer. This time, however, the shooter took his own life with a shot to the head with the same gun that had fatally wounded Jerrod on the sidewalk in front of Keiara's home.

After her brother's funeral, Keiara fell into a deep depression. The only consolation she allowed herself was a tattoo in honor of Jerrod's life, a Leo horoscope sign on her right forearm. She reverted to the person she was after being raped. She shut herself off emotionally from her friends and family and headed to the stables on a daily basis. Her horse Skip, the same horse she had owned since she was fifteen, again became a sounding board for her pain.

It had been a year since she last rode, and the death of her brother was the inspiration she needed to begin riding again and dreaming about competing in rodeos. Dropping out of college

ANTHONY is at home with his granddaughters. He rode his horse to pick one of them up at school. He tends to do this on Fridays. They are in the Imperial Courts housing projects in Watts, California.

ANTHONY is at his granddaughter's elementary school in Watts, California. All of the kids are petting his horse, Dakota. He rode his horse from the Richland Farms ranch. It took about thirty minutes to get to the school.

ANTHONY is having a moment with his horse, Dakota, on the Richland Farms ranch. He works at the ranch every day from 5 a.m. to 12 p.m. Anthony takes care of all the horses, but he has the strongest bond with Dakota.

ANTHONY is washing Dakota in the driveway. Every cowboy contributes to the grooming of the horses.

CARLTON HOOK is posing for a photograph on the Compton Cowboys' ranch. This photo was taken after he finished feeding the horses one early afternoon.

COMPTON COWBOYS members Charles Harris and Randy Hook are sitting on their horses during the middle of the Compton Christmas Parade.

MEMBERS OF THE COMPTON COWBOYS attend fellow cowboy, close friend, and Richland Farms native, Slim's funeral during the summer of 2018.

CARLTON HOOK, KEENAN ABERCROMBIA, AND KENNETH ATKINS wait for their order of food to arrive from the local Louisiana Fried Chicken restaurant in Compton, California. *(New York Times)*

MEMBERS OF THE COMPTON COWBOYS wait for the rest of the group to arrive so they can ride together in the Compton Christmas Parade.

KEENAN ABERCROMBIA gets ready to start his day in the bathroom mirror.

KEENAN washes dishes in his mother's home.

KEENAN rides through the streets of Compton, California.

KEENAN ABERCROMBIA poses for a photograph with his stepdaughter.

KEIARA poses for a photograph with her daughter, Taylor.

KEIARA AND HER DAUGHTER, TAYLOR, ride around the stables in nearby, Gardena, California.

KENNETH stands on the corner with his horse, Ebony, while the light turns green.

KENNETH waits for the light to turn green on his horse, Ebony. They are standing on the intersection of Wilmington Avenue and Alondra Boulevard.

RANDY HOOK AND KENNETH ATKINS ride through the streets of Compton, California.

RANDY poses with his son, Lux.

RANDY HOOK puts on his cowboy hat in his home in the Richland Farms before attending the PBR event in downtown Los Angeles, California.

TRE HOSLEY is breaking a horse in in Kenneth's backyard stable while his friend watches on.

TRE HOSLEY, a part-time barber, cuts Keenan's hair near the ranch's riding arena.

TRE HOSLEY takes a break from practicing with other local black cowboys in Palos Verdes, California.

TRE HOSLEY'S championship saddle.

TRE HOSLEY tends to one of his horses on the Richland Farms ranch.

wasn't her plan, but neither was coming back to Compton to bury her brother. After working the horse early in the mornings, she would take him out on daily walks around the same neighborhood where she and her brother had grown up. The walks became healing and therapeutic. Each one was an opportunity to think about what she could have done differently. If only Jerrod would have committed his life to horses like she did, she believed he would still be alive.

One morning, though, at the corner of Broadway and 134th Street, her horse's breath began to pick up and his knees began to wobble. He shook uncontrollably, forcing Keiara to jump off the saddle and into a thorny bush. Moments later, Skip collapsed in the middle of the street. Keiara placed her hand under his nose, hoping to feel his breath, but there was nothing. She yelled Skip's name as her horse's eyes suddenly began to roll into the back of his head, and within moments he lay lifeless in the street, a few blocks away from where her brother had been killed just one month before.

The intersection of Broadway and 134th Street had historically been a popular murder location. It was just blocks away from Athens Park, home to the infamous Athens Park Bloods, one of the most notorious Blood gangs in Los Angeles. Dead black bodies on the street became the norm. A dead horse on the street, however, drew more attention.

Keiara took off her boots and began to weep in front of the crowd that had gathered next to her horse. She sat on the curb and thought about the deaths of her brother and her horse. Two of the most important things in her life had been taken from her.

While she was picking out her brother's grave lot only weeks before, two butterflies had flown onto her shoulder and remained perched there for several minutes. Butterflies had always been one of her favorite animals. They symbolized a fresh start and a sense of transformation following death or loss. Seeing both of them surprised her. Perhaps one of them represented her brother, she thought. As she sat on the curb looking at her dead horse, she realized that the second butterfly represented the death of Skip, her other best friend.

TIME HAD HEALED some of the wounds that Keiara experienced as a child. Though she was back in the same neighborhood that had brought her pain, she was also in the place that brought her the most joy. Being away from Compton helped her understand that there was a world outside of her neighborhood, and that she needed to heal from some of the wounds she had experienced. As a twenty-nine-year-old single mother, Keiara believed that the amount of death she had experienced in her lifetime had prepared her for the next two years.

Her brother had been the one person in her life who continued to motivate her to ride and compete. Being the first black woman to win a national barrel racing competition would be the only way to honor his life.

A few days after Skip's death, while digging through her closet, she stumbled on a barrel racing book. It was dusty and missing pages, but reading it was like a sign from God—it could help her become the champion she knew she'd once felt destined to be. She turned the first page.

The death of her brother and her horse had sent Keiara to a dark place. Years of unresolved childhood trauma had manifested in depression and insomnia. She self-medicated with alcohol like others in her family had done. She began drinking Patrón tequila whenever she got a chance and smoked weed heavily for months. During the weekends she sometimes went through two or three bottles, each taking her away from the pain, but closer to the darkness of addiction that she had seen in her family and that she had always feared for herself.

One day, Keiara decided to look for a therapist she could talk to about drinking and ongoing depression. It was the first time anyone in her family had sought out therapy. Her grandfather frowned upon it, and some of her friends wondered aloud if she was losing her mind. But seeing a therapist and speaking about her brother's death in the year after he was killed taught her more about herself than she had ever known. The turmoil she felt made sense in the context of every childhood trauma that she had experienced. She learned that the uncontrollable fits of rage that she experienced around people were a symptom of suppressed feelings. She learned about boundaries and began establishing them with her parents, whose behavior had been triggers in her life.

Still, Keiara continued to wake up in the mornings and cry uncontrollably. Something was missing, and the potential answer to her problems had four legs. Her therapist helped her realize that horses had been her escape as a child and reconnecting with them would be beneficial. Her new horse, Penny, could be the answer to her turmoil.

Penny wasn't like the horses Keiara had previously owned. She was the color of a chestnut, stable and calm, and didn't buck when she tugged on her reins. With time and with more practice she believed they could become a great team. Penny was more than just an opportunity for her to get back into the barrel racing circuit. The horse taught her how to be tender again. Horses don't respond to aggressive energy, so he made her check her anger and confront the reasons why she took her anger out on people. Penny softened her.

Penny also taught her about communication. Learning to be around an animal that doesn't speak forced her to tune in to a part of her body that she had forgotten how to use since she was a teenager. She began to listen to her horse and, by extension, herself.

Within a year, Keiara was back on her horse and communicating in ways that she never imagined. She started a women's group called Women Unity that met once a month at her cousin's home in North Long Beach to make sense of her pain and that of those around her. Many of the women in attendance were also single mothers who for the first time in their lives spoke openly about anxiety and depression. The weekly meetings became healing circles that allowed her to share things that she had only shared with the horses she had owned throughout her life. She spoke openly about the sexual abuse, her temper and anger, and her mental health. It all began to make sense. Her sporadic angry flare-ups were rooted not only in the generational trauma that she had inherited as a child, but also the events she had experienced in her life. The migraines that began in the fourth grade that used to leave her incapacitated were caused by the stress she experienced at home.

Getting back to her training regime was the most important thing for Keiara. As the only woman in the Compton Cowboys, it was her goal to help other black women become more involved in the sport. Barrel racing tended to be the only event offered for women at rodeos, while men could choose between team roping, calf roping, bull riding, steer wrestling, and bronco riding. Black rodeos, in particular, were smaller in scale but usually offered women the choice between lady steer riding and undecorating, two events involving bulls that never interested Keiara.

Still, getting healthy would be her toughest challenge. Injuries continued to plague her recovery. In July, while she was driving through Compton, a car crashed into her vehicle's bumper, immediately sending a sharp pain through her entire back. That night, when the adrenaline wore off, she fell into bed and had trouble standing. A visit to the doctor's office revealed that she had suffered four badly swollen intervertebral discs in her upper and lower back. God had such an interesting way of testing her, she thought while examining the X-rays with her doctor. She would have to be off of her horse for at least another three months. Though her doctor had sternly advised her not to ride or do anything that might affect her recovery, she still had to care for her daughter, feed her horse, and also look after her grandmother and earn a living as a caregiver for the elderly and disabled.

Keiara continued living through the pain, one day at a time.

CLOSE CALL

THE LATE AFTERNOON TRAFFIC ZIPPED past Keenan as he rode on the Wilmington Avenue sidewalk while Kenneth and Carlton trailed closely behind on their horses.

Since moving to Inglewood with his wife and her daughter, Keenan had spent less time on the ranch. His work schedule and his suspended license made it challenging to find time for the horses like he used to. Riding had helped him deal with the pressures brought on by a sometimes sixty-hour workweek, but without the horses, alcohol became his chosen stress relief.

Their horses' ears and tails were perked high above their heads, signaling slight danger as cars continued to speed only a few feet away from them.

"Remember the last time we were at Louisiana's and them niggas from Nutty's was over there?" Kenneth asked while loosening Ebony's reins. He glanced over his left shoulder to make sure he was heard. "Remember when we seen them niggas from Nutty that one time?"

"Yeah," Carlton responded while looking west in the direction of the Nutty Blocc territory. "What you think would have happened if we wasn't on the horses?"

"What you think would have happened?" Kenneth sarcastically responded. "We for damn sure wouldn't be riding here today."

The Nuttys had been at war with the Farm Dog Crips for decades, and in most situations, walking through their territory to Louisiana Fried Chicken would have been a death wish. But on top of the horses, the three childhood friends felt invincible, like real-life 'hood superheroes.

At this point in their lives their horses were able to sense danger long before they could. The farm's horses had developed a sense for survival, and if the animals didn't feel safe, they would stop and turn around. While the horses guaranteed some safety, the past hadn't always. Over the years, some members of the Nuttys had shot at riders from the farms whom they suspected of being members of the Farm Dogs.

At the end of the day nobody was really safe.

Keenan's horse, Sonny, had been especially jumpy during the entire ride. He sensed Keenan's own anxieties about riding so close to the Nuttys' neighborhood and tensed up at every car that passed. Part of Sonny's nervousness had to do with the abuse he experienced as a young colt and the lasting fear caused by a plastic toy water gun that went off near his ear over five years earlier.

"These horses saved us," Carlton replied with a southern drawl as he rode with one hand on his rein while using the other to send a message on his phone. "They was trippin' but we got away 'cause we had the horses with us."

The afternoon wind began to pick up, making Keenan wish he had worn more than a basketball jersey, jeans, and blue Nike Air Jordan shoes to ride in. The traffic increased as commuters filled Wilmington Avenue on their way home from work.

Louisiana Fried Chicken was a neighborhood favorite. It was only a ten-minute ride from the ranch and easy to get to using back streets. If it wasn't Louisiana's it was Mom's or Cliff's Burgers on Alondra Boulevard, where they didn't have to get down from their horses to order their food.

Keenan got off his horse, tied Sonny to the pole, and walked through the front doors of Louisiana's. A child with two braids in her hair eagerly looked through the window while Kenneth and Carlton waited outside, still mounted on their horses. The little girl looked at them like she had never seen horse riders with the same color skin as her. She pressed her face tightly against the inside of the glass and waved at the horses as if hoping they would wave back.

Behind the heavily protected plexiglass, a Louisiana manager had other feelings about the horses. "Who gonna clean up all that shit y'all leaving outside?" she brashly confronted Keenan through the old speaker system. "I hope you don't think you just gonna come here, have your horse shit everywhere, and then ride away like nothing happened? You got me fucked up!"

Keenan and the other customers inside the restaurant laughed. The only person who didn't laugh was the manager.

"You serious?" he asked.

"Hell yeah, I am."

"Alright, I'll pick it up on my way out."

"You better," she said.

After his order arrived, Keenan walked out of the restaurant and saw a pile of fresh green manure coming out of Sonny's rear end. It slowly piled onto another fresh heap that Sonny had left minutes before.

"Mothafucka," Keenan slowly said to himself while still holding his bag of food. "Why you gotta do me like that, Sonny?"

He looked around for something to pick up the droppings, but failed to find anything big enough to scoop it with. Horses produce almost fifty pounds of droppings a day, and in that moment it felt like all fifty had just come out of Sonny's rear end.

"What you gonna do?" Kenneth asked Keenan, laughing and looking at the manager, who was now standing by the glass using her arms to simulate a shoveling motion.

"I guess I gotta pick up this shit with my hands," he said.

A crowd of people gathered around Keenan as the face-off between the manager and the cowboys drew in other members from the community. Cars passed through the major intersection honking and yelling in support of the cowboys.

"Yeeeeeehaw!" someone yelled from a passing truck. "Yeeeee-haw!"

After a few minutes of internal deliberation, Keenan finally dug both of his hands into the droppings and carried them to a nearby trash can. Some people contorted their faces in disgust, while others gathered around to laugh at the scene. It wasn't every day that you saw a grown man pick up horse shit with his hands in Compton.

"Put some of this shit in your combo meal," Keenan told someone who laughed on their way out of the restaurant. "It'll give it a nice flavor." He brushed his hands off on his pants, saddled back up, and started riding in the direction of the ranch.

After a few minutes of riding, Sonny began to feel uneasy and continued to fight Keenan. Then a red car pulled up near the group and honked its horn, startling Sonny and sending him into a panic. On the second honk, Sonny bolted south on Wilmington Avenue, taking Keenan with him and leaving the rest of the group in the distance. He picked up speed as all four of his hooves floated off the ground for what seemed like seconds at a time.

Keenan attempted to regain control by pulling hard on the reins and squeezing his legs around the horse, but Sonny was frantic now, and refused to stop.

"Sonny, come back!" Kenneth and Carlton yelled as Sonny continued galloping uncontrollably down Wilmington Avenue.

The three friends and their horses were now sprinting through the streets like the cowboys of days past. In the old West, their horses would have run as a way to evade danger, but in this situation it seemed like Sonny was running toward it.

The sight of three young black men running on foot at full speed through the streets of Compton would have elicited a different reaction from bystanders and pedestrians, who would assume they were running from the police or a rival gang. Three black men going full speed on horses, however, almost felt like an optical illusion.

As Sonny continued to dash along the sidewalk, visions of Flower raced across Keenan's mind. Flashbacks of her dying body on the asphalt haunted his every stride.

He yelled louder.

But his yells were drained out by the sound of Sonny's hooves. Part of Keenan felt like the uncontrollable nature of the moment was a metaphor for the life he had lived growing up: fast and daring and potentially fatal. It almost seemed poetic to die on a horse.

But while those images immediately jolted into his mind, images of his wife and her child—the daughter he had vowed to help raise—also consumed him.

Keenan was left with no choice. In a matter of seconds, Sonny would crash into the oncoming Wilmington traffic and take him along with him. Keenan could either brace himself for the collision or he could jump off the horse and try to guide him away from the cars.

"One . . . two . . . three," he counted in his head before finally jumping.

He landed in between Sonny and the cars, acting as a protective barrier between his horse and the oncoming traffic, and slapped Sonny's rear and yelled into his ear as the horse screeched to a stop.

"Why the fuck did you do that, Sonny?" he yelled. Carlton and Kenneth caught up to them. Keenan panted and bent at his waist to catch his breath. He continued to grab on to the saddle like his life depended on it.

"You could have fucking died, Sonny!" he yelled. "You could have fucking died!"

The three friends rode their horses home in silence, avoiding eye contact and conversation. Near-death moments were always followed by deep introspection. It was the way of the farms.

GOOD KID

"NEXT UP TO SPEAK TONIGHT is Randy Hook, a member of the Compton Cowboys," the council member said through a microphone. "You have three minutes to speak, sir." The city council chamber was filled with a variety of Compton residents. Some were there to speak, others to listen to the council's plans for the community.

In recent years the city of Compton had been under investigation for a series of corruption scandals, which broke the trust of the community. Now local officials were fighting hard to regain it. As a child, Randy had watched Mayisha speak at council hearings on countless occasions. She had always been an advocate for more resources for the Richland Farms, and her confidence boomed throughout the room, making him proud to be her nephew.

As he approached the podium for the first time, he thought about the big shoes that Mayisha had left for him to fill. He was the youngest speaker that night and had a vision for his community that was centered on developing more horse programs for Compton's youth. At one point in his life, Randy had a dream of entering politics—the reason why he chose to major in sociology in college. He stroked his beard and then adjusted his black Stetson hat in front of the mostly middle-aged African-American and Latino residents. All eyes were on the lone cowboy in the room.

"Good evening, everyone," he said. "My name is Randy Hook

and I am a member of the Compton Cowboys. We're a group of horse riders from the Richland Farms and I'm here to speak about the need to put more resources into the farms. Horses are a big part of the community and we think they could really help with the image of the city. As residents of the Richland Farms, we've been asking for more horse-riding lanes on the streets, and we need to have cleaner trails by the canals."

Members of the council leaned forward in their seats and listened. Randy's cowboy hat, gold earrings, and nose ring raised some eyebrows. Council members adjusted their glasses and took down detailed notes as he spoke. Randy's speech captivated them, but he secretly thought entering the room while mounted on his horse would have created more of a splash.

He spoke about the power that horses continued to have on youth on the farms and the changes he had seen in them. But without the help of the city, the impact of their program would be minimal. Many of Compton's own residents weren't aware that the farms existed, and he wanted to change that. He wanted a designated trail throughout the city and signage that detailed the farms' geographic boundaries. There was also a need to clean up and clear areas that had been neglected for too long, where debris and overgrowth prevented horse riding.

When his three-minute session ended, the council vowed to allocate more resources to the farms and to schedule a cleanup effort over the next few weeks.

"Thank you for listening," Randy said.

For many of the council members, it was their first time interacting with the new generation of black cowboys from the farms. The idea of young black men on horses was tough for some of them to fathom. Most young black men at Randy's age were either in prison or involved with gangs.

The meeting established Randy as the voice of the Compton Cowboys and their neighborhood, a part of the city that sometimes wasn't recognized even by its own. His decision to begin attending council meetings had been spurred by recent conversations that he had begun with other members of the cowboys. "We have to put the same energy on the community-building side of things as we do with the riding and entertainment side of things," he had said to them in a group chat text. "What good does it do if we don't help our community?"

Finding ways to give back was an ongoing issue for the group. Randy understood that the ranch had been established as a way to give back to the farms' community. As Mayisha's nephew, he understood that her dream had been a program that would put children's needs at the very center. Everything else was secondary.

At the same time, he also understood the challenges that came with that model. Mayisha had had wealthy financial donors throughout the years, while the Compton Cowboys had none. Perhaps it was the move to get back to their roots of western riding that alarmed wealthy white donors. Riding western directly invoked the forgotten history of black cowboys in the West. It was as much a political choice as it was a cultural choice. Riding western came with less outside funding and resources than the more elitist English style. Now they were on their own and would have to fend for themselves to inspire more interest in the Compton Cowboys. For many of the cowboys, it felt like their own community didn't believe in their ability to successfully run the ranch. At times it felt like they were being set up for failure. Still, Randy hoped that moving back to the more popular western riding would bring in more kids from the streets.

Most of Randy's time these days was spent trying to reestablish the ranch's presence in the community. New riders needed to be recruited, and every day was a struggle to secure meetings with potential sponsors and donors. The Los Angeles Chargers, the Professional Bull Riders, Dr. Dre—they were all on his list. If the ranch could have a chance to survive, the cowboys would have to secure immediate funds to help jump-start the new five-pillar program that he developed: Education, Business, Athletics, Guidance, and Therapy. He was even learning the most basic steps—filing taxes, incorporating a company. Running a business and philanthropic group wasn't something he'd learned growing up. He was doing the best he could with the little he had.

SINCE MOVING BACK to the farms last year, Randy had struggled to find balance both in himself and in the community. He had left Compton to go to college and then moved to the San Fernando Valley to live with the mother of his child.

But being back home came with a rude awakening. He began to feel the pressures of the streets in ways that he didn't understand as a teenager. That also reaffirmed for him the effect the ranch could have to heal an entire community. He believed the ranch had the power to save everyone. Even with the group acting like a dysfunctional family and the community having its own challenges, there was real love there, and they needed the ranch to nourish it.

Being at the helm of the ranch also meant that Randy had to confront personal challenges and find ways to rise above them. Mental illness had plagued his family for generations; one of his aunts had committed suicide as a result of symptoms related to schizophrenia and bipolar disorder. He considered his own family dysfunctional, like many of the black families he knew in Compton, and the mental health problems only made things harder. His aunt's suicide was the most extreme example, but he recognized a form of the illness in everyone in his family. They all had the same kind of emotional instability and anger problems, and yet none of them knew where the hell it stemmed from.

As an adult Randy had attempted to address his condition by seeking therapy, but at this point in his life—with the responsibility of keeping the ranch afloat—his own healing was put on the back burner.

When things began to pick up with the cowboys, Randy found it hard to sleep at night. Insomnia had been a frequent visitor throughout his life, but at twenty-eight and with the pressures of keeping the ranch alive, it had kicked into high gear.

As Randy drove through the city following the council meeting, the sounds of Kendrick Lamar's album *Good Kid, M.A.A.D City* played loudly. His full beard, gold earrings, and nose ring moved together in unison while he bopped his head to the rhythm.

He drove through the city to find peace of mind and often found it in Kendrick's lyrics. He was brought to tears the first time he heard Kendrick's music in the driver's seat of his father's Toyota Camry. Keenan sat in the passenger seat and closed his eyes and took in the Compton rapper's words in the same way. After listening to the song on repeat, they both sang:

> When the lights shine off and it's my turn to settle down,
> my main concern, promise that you will sing about me,
> promise that you will sing about me,
> promise that you'll sing about me.

Both Randy and Keenan had grown up listening to rap groups like N.W.A but had never had someone speak to them the way

Kendrick's music did. His music provided a soundtrack for their lives in ways that no other musician had done before. Kendrick understood what it was like growing up in the 'hood, and many of the traumas and everyday struggles he experienced were Randy's and Keenan's too. Also, like Kendrick, they had grown up eating at Louis Burgers on Rosecrans, and both navigated through the same situations with girls that Kendrick often rapped about. They both also considered themselves good kids in a mad city.

Kendrick's music spoke to them in a way that the older generation of Compton rappers like Eazy-E and Dr. Dre could not. They were all dodging the same bullshit that came from growing up in the 'hood, and they were the same age and from the same generation. Kendrick inspired Randy to consider what kind of influence the ranch could have outside of Compton. He hoped to create bridges between other black cowboys around the United States by adopting similar youth ranch programs in other urban cities. It could be the start of a movement. If horses could work in Compton, they might work in other neglected urban communities as well. There were black cowboys in Philly, black cowboys in Chicago, and new groups popping up in just about every American city. It was making such an impact here, he thought, why not spread it elsewhere? It could be the prototype for all other 'hoods in America.

The dream of uniting the Compton Cowboys with other black riding communities was both palpable and a challenge. Social media had allowed the cowboys to connect with other riders, and as each day passed, more and more black cowboys from around the country began to contact him about the need to create more programs for black youth riders. The incentive to create more riding programs felt especially urgent as the killings of unarmed black men by police officers continued to occur throughout the

United States. Randy believed that the ranch could serve as a model to help decrease the violence. Black Lives Matter was about camaraderie and caring for other black people. It was the social justice movement in this political moment, and these horses, Randy felt, could help save black lives too.

DEATH OF A FLOWER

SONNY'S HABIT OF BOLTING WAS becoming increasingly dangerous for both him and Keenan. Part of being urban cowboys was the reality that riding through the streets came with serious risks. Since the streets of Compton didn't have designated riding areas, accidents happened frequently. For Keenan, who had once lost a horse to the streets, his fears for Sonny were mixed with memories that were sometimes too much to bear.

As a fourteen-year-old, Keenan hadn't minded when Carlton and Yaya hogged his video games in his room. Playing Madden was a sacred tradition and seeing both of them fight and argue about the score was always a highlight of his week. Besides, every time they played, they smoked, and amid their competitive zeal, they would forget about the weed that was being passed around.

"Shit, more for me," Keenan thought to himself as the blunt continued to dwindle between his fingers.

Carlton and Yaya had been playing video games in his bedroom for the past hour after getting home from summer school. The June sun was beginning to slowly set on Keenan's two-bedroom wooden home. It was a quiet afternoon, just loud enough to hear distant noises, but quiet enough to hear the creaking of the old house.

"Touchdown, mothafucka!" Carlton yelled into Yaya's face. "You can't see me, nigga!"

The afternoon light always found a way into the home's west-facing window, illuminating a series of horse paintings and figurines inside. An older photograph of an eight-year-old Keenan wearing a green Oakland A's baseball cap standing in front of his former East Oakland apartment building hung on the wall. Other photos of the Abercrombia family hung on the walls next to it. A photo frame of Keenan's grandmother, a Creole woman from Louisiana, stood by the front door. Another photograph of his sister the day she graduated from veterinary school hung proudly near the front door entrance. On the south wall was a pair of first-place medals that Keenan had earned at the Palos Verdes equestrian competition in middle school. Each marked a cherished memory.

Before Keenan and his mother moved to the home located in between Mayisha's and Louie's, they had been living on couches throughout Los Angeles. The move from Oakland had not gone as smoothly as Keenan's mother had hoped. Rent was more than she could afford and landlords required first and last month's rent at a time when super-sizing a meal at McDonald's was a struggle for the young family. So they lived on couches with friends and relatives until someone they knew proposed moving into an affordable home on a horse ranch in Compton. For an animal lover like Keenan, that had sounded like a dream come true. The chance to live in a home and be around animals was an opportunity his mother could not pass up.

Carlton and Yaya continued to laugh and stomp on the brown carpet floor, worrying Keenan that they might wake up his mother, who slept during the day and worked the graveyard shift at the airport at night.

"Niggas, please keep your voices down, my mom's sleeping in the other room," he pleaded. "You remember how mad she got the last time we woke her up?"

His house phone rang loudly in the living room, but the sound of the video game and their conversations made it hard to hear. The fifth time it rang, Keenan heard it and jumped off his bed and walked out of his room.

"Who could be calling right now?" he thought to himself. The creditors with the funny Midwestern accents usually harassed them earlier in the morning and the older women from church didn't call until around 6 p.m. Maybe it was his girlfriend, Tamra, who usually called during her fifteen-minute break at work from Hot Dog on a Stick.

He picked up the phone and saw that he had four missed calls from Tre. As a member of the Farm Dog Crips, four missed phone calls meant that a close friend or relative was in a bind and in need of immediate help.

Or, worse, it could mean that someone had just gotten shot or killed.

"Keenan, it's me," Tre said immediately after a short delay. "Come to Oleander and Caldwell."

"What?" Keenan asked.

"Something just happened to your horse," Tre said in a soft and distant voice. "Hurry up."

"Flower?" Keenan asked. "What the fuck happened to my horse? I left her in her stall at Tracey's house, man," he shouted back at Tre, no longer concerned about his mother waking up.

"Man, I can't explain over the phone. Just come quick, man," Tre said before hanging up.

Keenan put the phone back on the receiver, threw on a pair of blue Nike low-top cross trainers, and bolted out of his front door, still wearing the same white tank top and basketball shorts he had been wearing the entire day. He slammed the iron security door behind him, rattling the entire home, and blindly sprinted toward Oleander Avenue without knowing what awaited him, never even pausing to survey the street for enemies.

All he could think about was Flower as he sprinted past Mayisha's house, past Mr. William's home, and past Robert F. Kennedy Elementary School, toward the intersection of Caldwell and Oleander. The falling sun beat on the back of his neck while he continued to run. Drops of perspiration began to build up on his body as each arm swing and stride pumped adrenaline through his veins.

When he finally got to Oleander, he was met by a police officer who was redirecting traffic away from the middle of the street. A large crowd had gathered behind the officer, but Flower was nowhere to be found, only geometric shapes outlined by white chalk on the black asphalt. A few yards away two pieces of what looked like a car bumper were circled by the same white chalk. Nearby, another piece of a car bumper was also ringed with chalk.

As he approached the scene, another officer was busy unfolding a large white body bag from the trunk of his car. Still no sign of Flower.

Keenan finally pushed through the crowd of black and brown people to see that everyone's eyes were focused on a large mass on the ground.

It was a familiar scene that had played out in the community many times before. Only this time it wasn't a human body; it was his best friend and horse, Flower, a reddish-brown Arabian with white stripes and a white star on the ridge of her nose.

Flower's body quivered on the hard ground as she gasped for air. It had been nearly thirty minutes since she had been hit by an SUV in an apparent hit-and-run accident. The sound of her breath and pulsing of her heart suggested that she was minutes away from closing her eyes for the last time.

In Keenan's presence, Flower had always been calm, despite the abuse she had experienced before she arrived at the farms. But even Keenan's soothing demeanor could not quell the pain and fear that ran through her body now. She looked at him with the eyes reserved for someone whose love had been deeply betrayed.

Keenan refused to make eye contact. He felt guilt and shame. Worse, he felt like he had failed on the promise he had made to protect her when he bought her for a hundred dollars at a horse auction.

Behind him, a few bystanders explained how a midsized SUV had been recklessly speeding through the farms before its front bumper violently collided with Flower's right leg, severing it and sending it twenty feet away from the rest of her body. Eyewitnesses remembered hearing the truck hit the brakes, followed by a loud thud that could be heard from blocks away.

"The truck just hit the horse and drove off," one person said. "We heard a loud boom."

Flower bled profusely next to Keenan, as two dark puddles formed on the ground. Her muscles erratically convulsed after every breath she took. Somebody told Keenan that Chuck, an older rider from the neighborhood, had taken Flower out for a walk without Keenan's permission. He arrived minutes later, attempting to explain what had happened.

"I'm sorry, man," Chuck repeated three more times. "I'm sorry, man . . . I'm sorry, I'm so sorry."

Keenan didn't want to hear it.

Chuck had broken one of the most important codes on the farms: you do not ride someone else's horse without its owner's permission. His repeated attempts to console Keenan and amend the situation by offering him $250 only made Keenan more furious.

"You think that's going to bring my horse back to life? Two hundred and fifty dollars!" he yelled in Chuck's face. "What the fuck is wrong with you?!"

He turned away and knelt down to rub Flower's long jawline. Tre made his way through the crowd of people, accompanied by Keenan's mother, and both put their arms around him in an effort to console him.

"It was never supposed to end this way, my nigga," Keenan said, drying his tears with the reverse side of his T-shirt. "Flower didn't deserve this shit. Why did she have to die the same way homies die? A drive-by."

"It's all fucked up," Tre said, and put his hand on Keenan's shoulder again.

Despite continuing to rub Flower's jaw, Keenan still refused to make eye contact with the dying animal.

One of the officers approached him. He was white, young, burly, and had a shaved head. "What do you want to do with your horse?" the officer asked.

Keenan silently stood up and looked at him.

"You have two choices," the officer continued. "We can either put her down now or you can pay to get her transported to a hospital. It's your call."

Keenan would later learn that the officer was a rookie on the police force, and he looked eager to use his firearm for the first time since firing it at the police academy. The officer hadn't seen much action since he had joined over a year ago.

Keenan ignored the officer's request for action and knelt down to rub Flower's coat again. Death always seemed to find a way to sit next to him. He was used to seeing men dying on the streets, but holding his horse as she gasped her last breaths brought him closer to death in a way that he had never experienced before.

"What you wanna do?" Tre asked Keenan, staring at the puddle of blood that had now formed around his white sneakers.

He had to make the toughest decision of his life.

After minutes of deliberating, Keenan responded to the sheriff with a silent nod, prompting his mother to walk back to her car to look for a pair of scissors. In the horse community, cutting a horse's tail before its death was considered a sacred act. It was believed that an owner could preserve the memory of its soul by keeping its tail.

She returned moments later with a pair of scissors and cut the brown tail, handing it to Keenan, who turned around and immediately began walking home, refusing to see Flower's death.

Before Keenan made a right on Caldwell Street, two blasts from the officer's twelve-gauge shotgun rang loudly behind him, echoing shock waves that could be heard throughout the farms. His legs gave out and he dropped to the pavement, sobbing uncontrollably.

FLOWER'S DEATH WOULD permanently change Keenan. She was his best friend and had been taken from him the same way the streets tended to settle scores: through violence. Seeing her lifeless body on the street, her terrified eyes searching for his, gave him permanent nightmares and affected his sleep for months. He'd often wake in the middle of the night, crying out her name, still seeing the dark blood on the pavement.

Keenan wanted revenge, but he didn't know where to find it. He stopped riding horses. He gave up being a cowboy. Flower's death put him on a path of destruction that led to robberies, shootouts, drug use, and violence toward anyone who stood in his path. Within months, he dropped out of high school and began spending less time on the ranch and more time with members of the Farm Dog Crips. He began to put in more work and "earned his stripes," committing a number of violent crimes against enemy gangs. He found family and acceptance in the other boys and men who were part of his gang, replacing the companionship he lost with Flower's death.

"Putting in work," as Keenan and his friends often called it, came with the hope of earning more respect from the gang elders, who acted like father figures and mentors. On any given day it could mean walking over to Compton High School to fight a group of students who had disrespected the Farm Dog Crips, accompanying his friends on drive-bys on enemy turf, or selling drugs for the older guys on the block, who would give him a cut of the sales.

While Keenan was gang-banging, he began to cook around his house. He specialized in omelets, cheeseburgers, and hot dogs, and eventually made his way to more complex dishes like jambalaya and gumbo, recipes he had learned from his mother. Cooking, in some ways, provided him with the outlet he had missed after Flower's death. It also made him well liked among his peers, who would flock to his house to taste his dishes. His evolution into "Chef Keenan" brought him some of the peace that he had found in horse riding, the beginning of a journey that would eventually bring him back to the ranch.

MAXED OUT

ZOE CONTINUED TO BE THE only thing standing between Kenneth Atkins and his second liquor store run of the day.

"Get the fuck out of the way, Zoe!" he yelled at the top of his lungs while mounted on Ebony.

Zoe was his long-snouted, black-and-brown-haired German shepherd. She had been barking at Ebony for the past ten minutes in front of the green gate that separated his home from the street. Kenneth's morning had already started on the wrong foot, and Zoe was only making things worse. By this time, minutes before noon, he would have already ridden to the convenience store to stock up on beer and tobacco blunt wrappers.

"Zoe!" he yelled loud enough for the neighbors to hear, while simulating a throwing motion with his right arm.

The two-year-old German shepherd jumped back and retreated toward the rosebushes that lined the gravel driveway, creating enough room for a smooth exit. Kenneth loosened the reins and gave Ebony a kick on her sides.

"Come on, Ebony, let's go!" he yelled, then at Zoe as he passed her, "Next time, I'm going to let her kick the shit out of you!" Ebony began to pick up speed, her hooves thudding hard on the empty paved street ahead.

Kenneth and his mother first had stumbled on the ranch by mistake when he was in middle school and a friend of his recommended a horse ranch in Compton as a way for him to be around other black riders.

"There's a ranch in Compton called the Hill where you ride horses with other black people," his friend Victoria said to him one day at school.

His mother, Susan, worried when he complained about the lack of black riders at his competitions. As a twelve-year-old his equestrian experience had been entirely white, and he expressed concerns about feeling uncomfortable being the only black rider at events. The idea of having Kenneth around other black riders excited the Atkins family. They believed it would help him develop friendships with other African-American riders his age.

Finding the ranch, however, was one of the biggest challenges. They were only given the cross streets for the horse ranch. "You can find the ranch on 131st and Figueroa," Victoria explained to Kenneth's mother.

While trying to find the ranch, they accidentally got off on the wrong exit and ended up on the southside of Compton, which resulted in an hour-long search to no avail. The family returned home. A week later a Google search with the keywords "black horse ranch Compton" brought the Compton Junior Posse to the top of the search bar.

It would be the ranch on Caldwell Street. Susan and Kenneth made plans to meet up with Mayisha and get the grand tour. Shortly after, the Atkins family decided to purchase property adjacent to the ranch, so sure were they that it needed to be a part of their daily life. It was a large enough property to own horses and build a home for their son to be around other black horse riders.

Ebony was one of the few Tennessee Walking Horses on the farms, and one of its fastest. She was part of a breed of horses that were first introduced in the southern United States. Tennessee

Walkers were known for their unique four-beat walking pattern. Their speed and elegance made them prized possessions among the horse-riding community.

Today, as he rode to the liquor store, the Compton sun shone brightly off Kenneth's chiseled brown torso, casting even shadows on both sides. The tattoos that covered the entire top half of his shirtless body each had a different story to tell. His first, the initials of his first and last names on the backs of his forearms, was done the day after he turned eighteen. A cross with clouds on his right shoulder came next, followed by the word "rebel" on the inside of his left arm. On the outside of his left arm, in bright red, was the image of a fully detailed Lamborghini being pursued by a police helicopter.

While each of his tattoos was important to him, two stood out. His "Los Angeles" bold inked tattoo with a city skyline background on the top of his stomach was the most visible and recognizable. The other was a hand-drawn set of three horses, two of which represented Ebony. The other was a tribute to the famous French general Napoleon Bonaparte, one of his childhood heroes because of his short stature and military prowess.

Tichenor Street was empty except for a few cars parked next to the wooden logs that separated the street from the road. Sylvester, Kenneth's neighbor, had been working on a piece of machinery in his backyard the entire morning, making sharp grinding noises as Kenneth rode past his home. Most of Kenneth's neighbors worked during the day and came home around the same time every evening. During the day, however, it was usually just Kenneth and Ebony riding around the farms.

A few men gathered outside their homes to watch Kenneth and Ebony as they rode in the direction of the liquor store. One of them waved, while others stopped to take photos. The sight of a black man on a horse riding bareback through the farms still fascinated many of the newly arrived Mexican residents.

"Hey, black cowboy!" said an elderly Latino man with a strong accent driving a van full of people next to Kenneth. "Alriiiiight," he said while pulling away, gesturing a thumbs-up. The children in the backseat waved and recorded him on their phones as the car sped off.

Kenneth never minded the extra attention he received when he rode around the farms without a T-shirt. Riding shirtless and without a saddle was to him the ultimate sign of rebellion. Every time he did it he felt like he flipped society off with both of his middle fingers. It fed into his bad boy image and, he believed, helped him with the ladies. "Every woman loves them a shirtless cowboy," he often said to the guys. "First, they go crazy over the horses. But when they see me without a shirt, it's a wrap."

Riding Ebony through the farms also reminded him of the cowboy westerns he used to watch with his older brother as a child. Even though the white cowboys tended to be depicted as the good guys, he always rooted for the Native Americans since the day his mother first mentioned that he had Cherokee blood on both sides of his family tree.

Kenneth pulled Ebony's reins to the right once they hit Center Avenue, next to a Spanish-style home with a large green cactus that stretched onto the street. He'd mastered the ability to simultaneously ride and text on his phone while listening to music on his headphones, bobbing his dreads to the lyrics of Young Dolph, his favorite rapper.

At this point, Ebony was Kenneth's only form of transportation. Earlier in the year he had nearly totaled his white Infiniti coupe on the 91 Freeway and picked up his second DUI. The accident served as an awakening; he had a problem and needed help. His reliance on alcohol worried everyone around him, especially his mother, who knew that alcoholism ran through both sides of his family and had affected the lives of his relatives in the Midwest for generations.

Without a car, Kenneth rode Ebony wherever he went, which brought them closer together and brought his mother some peace, knowing that her son wouldn't be driving on the streets.

On top of his latest bouts with alcoholism, Kenneth's troubles with KJ, Mayisha's grandchild, had started back up again.

Their problems stemmed from a transaction involving Eugene, the youngest cowboy on the farms, who was interested in purchasing KJ's mini motorcycle. Kenneth got wind of the asking price and accused KJ of trying to take advantage of the younger Eugene. A day later, KJ, who had just moved back to the ranch from Arizona, got into an argument with Carlton, his first cousin. He'd punched him in the eye, fracturing his eye socket. Kenneth rode over to KJ's home the next day and confronted him about the altercation.

Each altercation that followed began to involve more members of the Hook family, including KJ's father, Khafra, Randy, and Louie. A rift in the Hook family was emerging and Kenneth was caught in the middle of it. His intoxicated fits of rage almost always led him back to KJ's home to escalate the conflict, creating more concerns for the safety of the ranch.

As Kenneth rode Ebony west on Tichenor toward Center Avenue, his throbbing headache spread toward the back of his head. Just that morning, another round of fights with KJ had occurred. This time, KJ's father, Khafra, was involved. As Kenneth and KJ fought in front of their home, KJ's sister ran behind Kenneth and yanked two of his braids from his head, tossing them into the air while Kenneth's face continued to get pounded by KJ's fists.

The fight lasted for a few minutes before Anthony and Keenan, who had been working in the back of the ranch, heard the commotion and sprinted to the front of the ranch to break it up. A crowd of people from the neighborhood had gathered around them, leaving Ebony out of view. While they fought, she trotted away, only furthering the confusion Kenneth felt when he finally regained his senses and couldn't find her.

"I told him he didn't want none of me!" KJ yelled out as his sister and his father grabbed him from atop Kenneth's body. "I'm gonna max his ass out again if he ever comes back," he continued to yell to a growing group of people who had gathered outside his home. Although KJ was a teenager, he had the body of someone well into his twenties. He was stocky and the veins in his muscles stood out.

"Kenneth, get the fuck out of here!" Anthony yelled, shoving him in the opposite direction. "What the fuck is wrong with you? Get the fuck out of here."

"Where the fuck is my horse?" Kenneth finally asked while picking up what was left of his dreads on the ground. "Where the fuck did Ebony go?"

"She ran that way," Anthony said, pointing in the direction of Wilmington Avenue. "Go!"

A disoriented Kenneth ran to fetch Ebony with a series of new bruises on his head and less hair than he had woken up with that morning.

Something about this fight felt different from the rest of the altercations Kenneth had had with KJ. It seemed like a breaking point for the rest of the guys, particularly for Anthony, who had warned Kenneth not to go back to KJ's house ever again.

Anthony's patience was running low. Many of the cowboys already disliked Kenneth for the way he treated his mother and for the person he became when he drank. They also disliked the lifestyle he lived, regularly bragging about his riches and fame on social media while smoking 'woods.

On top of that, there were other, cultural differences that he had with the rest of the cowboys.

Kenneth was the son of hardworking parents who had acquired middle-class wealth and stability and had given him everything he wanted as a child. They owned homes in Ladera Heights, a middle-class African-American community in Los Angeles, and owned an elder care facility and the property located directly behind the ranch. Everyone on the ranch believed that his more affluent parents enabled Kenneth's antics by providing a rent-free home and a weekly allowance. Kenneth never had to hustle for what he wanted, much less commit crimes like most members of the cowboys. He was often resented for it.

"I'm done with him, man," Anthony told Keenan and Layton, who had just arrived, as they stood on Caldwell Street smoking Black & Mild cigars minutes after Kenneth rode away. "He needs to be out of the group."

"He has to go," Keenan replied.

"Yeah, he do," Layton said, nodding.

SITUATIONS LIKE THESE weren't rare for the cowboys. It wasn't the first time that Kenneth would be kicked out or suspended from the group. Randy was aware of Kenneth's transgressions, but he was also living in Kenneth's spare room. After living in his car, he had decided to move in with Kenneth. Now he struggled to confront his new roommate. The balance between acting as the Cowboys' manager and Kenneth's roommate wasn't easy. His reluctance to exclude Kenneth from the group's activities was not only widening the gulf between Kenneth and the group, but also raising questions about Randy's leadership. Kenneth had been suspended from the group on countless occasions, but now members wanted him to seek help for his alcohol problems or face permanent expulsion. They were on the edge and something had to change quick. Everyone's patience was running out.

Kenneth knew that his alcoholism was affecting the group's morale. He knew everyone was disappointed in him. He could feel the change in his body when he drank. When he wasn't drinking, he was just Kenneth—a loving, goofy, and joyful person to be around. He was the person everyone had fallen in love with when his parents first bought the land behind the ranch when he was eleven. But when he drank, he transformed into someone entirely different. He turned into Stona-man, his alter ego, a volatile version of himself that the group was starting to avoid.

Stona was cocky, brash, and disliked being proved wrong. Stona fought his father and verbally assaulted his mother, one of the people who cared for him the most. When he and his now-sober father fought, his father swung his fists at the person he once was, almost thirty years before: a raging and uncontrollable alcoholic on a downward spiral.

For Anthony, whose own mother had abandoned him as a child, seeing Kenneth argue with his mother on the ranch was triggering. Even when Kenneth and his mother argued inside their home, he could hear it and it bothered him. He couldn't bear the idea that someone could disrespect their own mother, especially given all that she continued to do for Kenneth.

"You can't speak to your mama like that, nigga," Anthony

would yell at Kenneth. "I never had a mother and you want to stand here and disrespect the woman who brought you into this world? I'm not gonna sit here and let that happen. Next time you speak to your mama like that I'm gonna fuck you up."

Every time Kenneth drank, he took a deep dive into a series of unresolved and crippling insecurities that he had faced as a child. He reverted to the wiry boy who was the victim of teasing and bullying because of his short stature and large protruding ears. When he drank, he overcompensated by performing a brand of toughness that he wished he had had when his bullies picked on him as a child. He became the braggadocious rappers that he watched on videos, boasting about the millions he didn't have while continuing to live from the allowance his parents gave him.

These were Kenneth's loneliest moments. The times when he was shunned by everyone he knew, returning to his only friends, the animals that he lived next to on the ranch.

KENNETH ARRIVED AT the liquor store to find Diego and a group of other homeless men drinking out of brown paper bags.

"Hi, gorgeous," Diego said, rubbing Ebony's coat and holding a large Bud Light beer can in his other hand. He was intoxicated and reeked of days-old alcohol.

The Asian woman who worked at the cash register didn't mind that Kenneth tied up Ebony in her parking lot. Nor that Ebony left enormous droppings in front of her store; Kenneth would be back in a few hours to purchase more alcohol, so she looked the other way. Besides, the store next door sold farm animal food and sometimes scooped it up to use as fertilizer.

When Kenneth was intoxicated, he had no concept of time. Sometimes he rode through the streets of Compton for hours, making stops at different liquor stores, marijuana dispensaries, and fast-food drive-thrus. His tattooed body stood out, particularly when he wore his red sandals and red sweats, which meant different things to different neighborhoods. Gangsters drove past him throwing up different gang signs, but the alcohol inside him made him numb and oblivious.

As he rode west on Alondra Boulevard on the sidewalk after stopping at the first liquor store, he suddenly steered Ebony's reins in the direction of the incoming traffic. He was fearless and numb after drinking several tall Bud Light cans to drown out the pain from the fight with KJ earlier that morning. The sun shone brightly on his face. He closed his eyes and rode into the intersection, didn't open them until the cars started honking.

"I don't give a fuck!" he yelled. "This is my fucking city!"

He had the look of someone who had reached a breaking point. Maybe it was time to end it all, he thought to himself as he loosened Ebony's reins and urged her to move forward while cars continued to honk and swerve in and out of the street.

"Dumbass!" someone yelled and flipped him off while driving past him.

He finally crossed the street and rode with the flow of traffic toward the intersection of Wilmington Avenue and Alondra Boulevard and the 7-Eleven convenience store, where other homeless men awaited him.

When he returned home from his store run, Carlton was sound asleep on his living room couch. His eye was still patched up from the force of KJ's fist days before. Outside, on the other side of his property, Kenneth's mother, Susan, was lamenting to Keenan.

"I think it's that stupid girl that he always hangs with," she said. They were standing under a wooden canopy near the bleachers that overlooked the ranch. "She always fucks with his head and he cries when she lies about coming and seeing him. That stupid bitch says she's coming over and then she never does. It's a trigger that really messes with his head."

Susan was convinced his ex-girlfriend was one of the main sources of Kenneth's drinking problem. Keenan nodded his head with his arms folded out in front of him. He listened intently to a part of the story that he had not yet heard.

"I thought about sending Kenny away from Compton for a while to seek treatment," she said in a solemn tone. "Then he stopped going to his job and started spending most of his days smoking and drinking."

Keenan nodded in agreement, kicked the dirt with his foot. He wasn't sure how to address the problem. He knew that the version they had all been seeing wasn't the boy he'd met when he was fourteen. He knew the real Kenneth and wanted him back like the rest of the cowboys did. "I've known him since he was fourteen," he said to Susan as a pack of dogs barked down the street. "I used to sleep over all the time and I know the real him—he can't keep riding this wave. It's going to get him killed."

Susan listened to Keenan and agreed that being a part of the Compton Cowboys was one of the few things that was keeping Kenneth from going over the edge. It was the only hope she had to save her boy from complete self-destruction.

"I'm worried that he's going to fuck up the whole Compton Cowboys thing," she said.

"Exactly," Anthony said as he dusted off the dirt from his work pants and walked up next to them.

"You guys have to have an intervention for him," his mother said. "But you have to do it when he's not drunk, because when he drinks he is out of control."

Anthony and Keenan silently nodded in approval.

"Because if not he's going to get hurt," she said as she wiped tears from her eyes, "he's going to either get killed or he's going to get seriously hurt, because he can be fucking crazy."

Susan's tears summoned deep feelings in Anthony. He reached over to hug her while thinking about his own complicated relationship with his mother, with whom he had reconnected in recent years.

"It's confusing for us, Susan, because when he drinks he wants to fight us and gets in our faces," Keenan said. "We're all friends and it should never come down to that, and then when he gets sober he always apologizes. We need Kenny back, the Kenny I used to know," he added, while Anthony nodded his head in agreement.

Keenan and Anthony worried that they would never see the old Kenneth. Part of them had already given up on him, but a small part of them believed that he could sober up and get control of his life again.

"You know Kevin, my husband, is from the South Side of Chicago and he doesn't play any games," Susan continued after a long pause in the conversation. "He was ready to evict him and hand him over to the police. But I fought him and said that he couldn't do that to my child. Kenny will tell me he's doing better and hasn't drank in five days, but then something will trigger him and will upset him."

"Oh, I didn't know that," Keenan said.

"It's that girl, I tell you, she just jerks him around."

"That shit fucks with his head," Keenan agreed.

"You guys have to save him. I've tried everything. Doctors, hospitals, clinics. You're his friends and he needs you," she said. "Yesterday he called me and told me he was scared and couldn't be by himself. He's not going to survive alone," she added. "He was bullied as a kid and had to develop a tough-guy image, he puts on this tough-guy persona when he drinks."

"That's when Stona comes out," Keenan said. "The tough guy, his alter ego."

"A fake-ass tough guy," Anthony chimed in. "He don't know what being tough really means. Shit, I was raised in these streets. He never had to do any of that. He never had to steal because he had no money. He never had to rob nobody's car. He don't know nothing about this life."

"When he turns into Stona, he disappears. And when we call him Kenny he won't respond," Keenan added.

"Maybe that should be part of the intervention," Susan said. "I'm not going to pay for thirty-day rehab and put up that kind of fucking money if he's not going to go to it."

"Right," Anthony said. "What's the point if he's not going to go to it?"

"That's a waste of money."

"We took him to one in Long Beach before. I had it all set up. Right on the beach where he could have run every morning if he wanted to. They were going to give him a scholarship but he had to detox, and two days in he blew up on someone in there. He thought he was only going to go for a day but then got angry when he realized he was going to sleep there."

Susan wiped more tears from her face.

"If he can get through the withdrawals then I think he has a chance to make it," she added.

DON'T MESS WITH TEXAS

"WELCOME TO EL PASO, TEXAS. Population 600,000," the sign read almost four years earlier. Tre slowed his car to a near halt and turned into a lane designated for passenger cars. The inspection station lights flashed brightly ahead as the colorful southwestern evening sky transitioned into complete darkness.

Tre briskly rubbed his goatee and stroked the back of his head after taking off his seat belt, preparing for the long wait. He had been accompanied for the past seventeen hours by Chris, a fellow rodeo competitor from Compton, who worked with him at the Flying U ranch, a stock ranch in Marysville, California. They were both on their way to the circuit rodeo finals in Texas, one of the most important events of the year, and were in good spirits after each having won their events at the California finals. Competing in the Texas circuit finals had been a goal for both riders; it was the crème de la crème of the rodeo world, and doing well there would help them move up in the rankings and put some extra money in their pockets.

The El Paso inspection point was one of the largest on Interstate 10 due to the high volume of vehicles from both sides of the U.S.-Mexico border. As many as one hundred thousand cars passed through it on a daily basis, and in recent years, border inspections had drastically skyrocketed as authorities tried to stanch the flow of drugs coming from Juárez, the Mexican city bordering El Paso, which suffered from one of the most notorious drug and crime cartels in North America.

On a good day, drivers would only be required to answer a quick citizenship question by border agents. "Are you a U.S. citizen?" agents would ask anyone suspected of being undocumented. If the color of your skin was brown, however, you would be asked to show your passport or other documentation. Vehicles that looked suspicious would be pulled aside, sometimes leading to lengthy searches.

After an hour of slowly inching forward in traffic and a series of intense debates about rodeo and football, Tre and Chris were finally within five cars of the checkpoint. Getting past the agent inside the inspection booth would mean one less barrier to achieving their dreams of winning big at the finals. As Tre softly pressed on the accelerator to move forward, an agent appeared in front of the cars ahead of him walking a drug-sniffing dog. The agent was young, perhaps his own age, with long dark hair. The dog on her leash was a basset hound, and it was heading in the direction of their car, sniffing and circling around each vehicle.

"You better not stop by this car," Tre said to himself under his breath while focusing his eyes on the dog's every move.

The dog walked up to Tre's side and immediately walked in a full circle, followed by a few quick nods to seize the agent's attention. The dog continued to aggressively sniff the outside of the vehicle before taking a seat and burrowing its paws on the ground near Tre's door.

"Gentlemen, I'm going to need you to slowly step out of your vehicle," the young Latina agent told Tre and Chris while calling for backup on her shoulder walkie-talkie. "Leave everything where it is and exit the car with your hands up."

Tre and Chris opened their doors.

"Slowly," the agent said while four nearby agents wearing matching black uniforms rushed to their car.

Tre kept calm as he stepped out of the car. He wasn't entirely surprised by the agent's request or the dog's suspicions. After all, they both had been smoking 'woods since they left Marysville more than three days earlier. To minimize the smell inside the rental car's polyester seats, they had rolled down the windows while clouds of smoke crept out after each exhale, which, as they later realized, did little to deter suspicion.

"What's this?" one of the agents asked Tre while holding the end of a fully smoked 'wood.

"It's exactly what you think it is," Tre replied nonchalantly.

"I think we got something here, guys," the agent said to the others.

A few minutes later, Tre and Chris sat handcuffed inside the inspection offices, next to a pair of African-American women who had been caught with a couple of grams of marijuana. All four of them waited in silence while a pair of officers filled out their paperwork.

Because they had been caught in a state with a zero-tolerance drug policy, Tre and Chris had immediately been put under arrest. If they had been caught in California, where marijuana had been legalized, they would have been released right away, but in a state with some of the most draconian drug policies in the country, even a small amount of marijuana could get you fined or, worse, imprisoned.

Luck, however, was on their side. The supervising sergeant let them off the hook by only issuing a $500 ticket without a mandated court date. The fine could be paid online and they could continue their journey to the rodeo finals.

The two women seated next to them, however, weren't as lucky. Because they were each found with several grams of marijuana, they would be taken to a local prison to be seen by a judge the next morning.

An hour later, Tre and Chris were out of handcuffs and back on the road. Though the ticket would cost them each $250, the situation, as Tre would learn, could have been worse. What the officers and dog did not find were the two ounces and packs of individually rolled 'woods that Chris had hidden inside one of his riding vests for the eleven-day trip. Had that amount of marijuana been found, both would have faced immediate jail time and sentences ranging from five to ten years.

After they stopped at a gas station to fill up and buy snacks, Chris walked back to the trunk and dug through his stash, pulled out a fresh 'wood and a lighter from the side compartment in his door, and victoriously sparked it, handing it to Tre as he drove off down the highway.

Each puff of the dimly lit 'wood calmed Tre from the stress that the inspection station had caused. It wasn't his first run-in with the police. As a teenager he had been in the back of several cop cars for fighting, but it was his first time being detained outside of Los Angeles. Within an hour Chris was sound asleep while Tre sipped on an iced tea and munched on a pack of M&M's that he carried on his lap.

As he burned the midnight oil, the excitement of competing at the circuit finals reentered his mind. That he and Chris had only walked away with a ticket following the fiasco in El Paso was a sign, he was sure, that he was supposed to have a successful rodeo. He thought about what he would do with his winnings. Maybe it was time to finally buy a new truck. He was tired of driving unreliable used trucks that often left him stranded on the side of roads.

Or maybe, with a big enough rodeo purse, he would be able to buy his own horses and breed them on the farms back in Compton.

Though Tre had emerged in recent years as one of the best black rodeo competitors in the country, rodeo was a relatively new venture for the high school and college football star. The idea of competing in rodeos had never crossed his mind until he was asked to attend the Southeast Texas Bareback Riding School four years earlier as a nineteen-year-old college football player. At that point, horses had been around his entire life. His father, also a rider, had introduced Tre to horses as a child, and he had fond memories of the rides they used to take during his youth. In middle school, his father signed him up with the Compton Junior Posse, which he was a part of until he decided to focus on football at Jordan High School, a high school located in North Long Beach.

Horse riding had been a hobby, particularly after Tre graduated from high school and was recruited to play at Cerritos College, a community college near Compton. Like his father, Andrew Hosley, who had also attended the same school and gone on to play collegiate football at Portland State, Tre excelled at football. As a cornerback, he loved the rush of hitting opposing wide receivers and became known throughout the city for his electrifying plays.

When he was introduced to competitive rodeo, however, a switch flipped. He felt the same thrill and adrenaline rush that he experienced as a cornerback. Rodeo events, like football stands, were also filled with adoring fans that he wanted to win over.

But leaving football would be difficult.

"You're going to fuck up," one of his football coaches told him when he shared the news that he was going to leave the team and pursue rodeo full-time. "If you have half the ability that your father had, you could be one of the best that we ever had. You're throwing away all of this ability."

Tre refused to budge. It was a decision that only he fully understood, so he remained strong while people teased and challenged him.

After deciding to leave football, Tre moved out to Texas and worked on a ranch owned by one of the most successful rodeo families in the United States. The family had met him while he was training at the camp and offered him a job and training. Though he was very raw and unrefined as a rodeo competitor, they saw potential in him. Working at their ranch was an offer that he couldn't refuse. Almost overnight the dream of being able to play in the National Football League was replaced by that of being able to compete in the Pro Rodeo Cowboys Association.

His style also evolved. He began to replace sneakers with boots and baseball caps with Stetson hats. If he was going to become a rodeo professional, he had better start looking like one, he thought.

Five years later, he drove down the same dark highway that first took him out of Compton to work in Texas.

AT 2:40 IN the morning, Tre looked over at Chris, still sound asleep. He kept his eyes on the road and noticed that an unknown vehicle's lights kept getting brighter and brighter in his rearview mirror. The car had been trailing him for the past hour and inching closer and closer as each minute passed. He tried to ignore it, writing the car off as just another bored hillbilly with nothing better to do than mess with drivers on the highway on a cold Thursday night.

He turned up the volume on his radio and manually lowered the window halfway, feeling the crisp breeze of the Texas night.

At the current pace, it would take him at least four more hours to reach the rodeo circuit finals in Waco. Chris had been asleep in the passenger seat since they last stopped at a gas station hours ago. The last 'wood Tre had smoked was long gone, but even though the back two windows were lowered, the smell continued to linger throughout the rental car.

As the unknown car continued to trail Tre, it crept closer and closer and, to Tre's astonishment, exposed what appeared to be objects on the roof that resembled police lights.

"Fuck," Tre said to himself, immediately straightening his posture and putting both hands on the wheel. "This motherfucking cop been on my ass this whole time."

The highway patrolman continued to follow Tre for a few miles, prompting him to make a brash decision. He could continue to drive on the highway and head toward his destination, or he could pull off at the next exit and attempt to lose the car. If the cop didn't follow him, they would be safe. But if he did, they would have to deal with the consequences. With a packed car full of rodeo gear, including horse tack, saddles, boots, ropes, gloves, and duffel bags full of clothes, he knew they could easily get off the hook by explaining the purpose of their trip. But he also knew that Texas highway patrolmen were known for stopping black drivers at random. On top of his fear of the cops, Tre also worried that they would find the two ounces of weed in their duffel bag.

In an act of desperation, Tre drove onto the slow lane, prompting the highway patrol car to immediately do the same.

"Aye, Chris, wake up, nigga," he said to Chris while repeatedly slapping his left shoulder. "Wake the fuck up, nigga, we're being followed by a cop."

"Huh?" Chris confusedly replied after being suddenly woken up. "What the fuck? Man, just keep driving and act normal."

Tre took the first exit off of the highway and made a right at the first light. Minutes after they exited, the police car's bright red lights lit up the night sky, followed by an order to pull over to the side of the road.

"Fuck," Tre said to himself, looking at the vehicle's lights through his rearview and side mirrors before pulling over. "Not again."

The highway patrolman and his partner exited their vehicle and immediately drew their guns.

"What are you guys doing?" an older white officer on Chris's side asked while pointing his firearm inches away from his face. "Where are you from and where are you going?" he said while looking at the car's California license plates.

"We're from California," Chris replied with his hands stretched out of the window and into the sky for the officer to see. "We're going to compete in a rodeo in Texas."

"Step out of the vehicle, gentlemen," the officers said as they backed away from the car, guns still drawn. One of the officers said that he could smell weed.

Tre cautiously stepped out of the vehicle and into the night. Both he and Chris were forced to place their hands behind their backs while the highway patrolmen handcuffed them. Their wrists were bruised, still sore from being handcuffed in El Paso just over four hours earlier. After they were read their rights, another officer showed up to the scene in a green police car, a veteran sheriff from a nearby county.

"Good evening, gentlemen," the white-haired sheriff said as he walked up to the group and picked up the marijuana capsule that one of the officers had placed on the trunk, inches away from Chris's handcuffed hands. "Looks like we got some of the green stuff."

Before the sheriff arrived, the young officers had thoroughly searched the inside of the car. There were dress shirts, cowboy hats, rodeo equipment, baseball caps, and boots that lay on the ground next to the car that the officers had removed from the backseat during their search.

"Oh, y'all rodeo?" one of the officers asked in a snarky tone while continuing to pull out rigs, cinches, and a latigo leather strap. The officers could hardly believe that Tre and Chris were cowboys.

"So, what you're telling me is y'all just some cowboys that smoke pot?" the sheriff asked as he weighed the situation. "Y'all just some cowboys that smoke pot?" he repeated again and again.

"Yeah," Tre said calmly.

Tre could tell that this sheriff was going to be their only way out of this situation. The younger officers were doing everything in their power to make sure Tre and Chris got the book thrown at them. Every few minutes one of them walked back to the car and asked about a certain piece of their equipment.

"What's this?" an officer asked forcefully.

"That's called rosin," Tre replied, looking at the white powder that was used to help with tighter grips. "We put that on our hands to help us control the grip on the rope."

"Don't be silly," the sheriff responded after each of the younger officer's queries. "That's absolutely nothing."

Their plans to make it to the circuit finals looked bleak, but at the very least they could get out of this situation the same way they had done in El Paso. The older sheriff continued to ask questions about rodeo while Tre eagerly entertained him. Chris stood by silently while the police car's lights shone brightly on their faces.

The more they spoke, the more Tre realized that the sheriff had had dreams of becoming a cowboy when he was a kid. Like most children in Texas, he had grown up watching old cowboy westerns and had vivid dreams of one day being able to ride off into the sun on the back of a horse.

After the rosin question, the sheriff ordered the younger officer to go in the squad car and work on his paperwork. He had had enough of his antics and decided to search the vehicle for himself. After all, in his mind, he was only dealing with a pair of pot-smoking cowboys who didn't present a threat.

He began searching one of Chris's bags in the trunk and opened it, flashed his flashlight inside it and then put it down. The sheriff's searches were nowhere as thorough as the younger officer's searches had been. He picked up Tre's bag and did the same. Nothing. The last bag he picked up was the one that held the two-ounce stash.

Tre could practically hear Chris's heart hit the ground when the sheriff opened the plastic rolling duffel bag. Chris had devised a plan for stashing his weed. He would lay his vest out and then place his chaps, pants, gloves, boots, and weed inside and then tightly close the vest up. It was a surefire way to hide the weed and keep the smell to a minimum. The officer took the vest out of the bag and began to unfold each item: first the chaps, then the pants, followed by the boots, and then he quickly put the vest back in the duffel bag and closed it.

Tre and Chris had evaded more serious charges for a second time. This time, however, they did have to spend a night in jail and see a judge in the morning. Like the situation in El Paso, they were forced to pay another ticket without doing any major jail time. The real problem had nothing to do with the weed they had been caught with. After being taken back to their impounded vehicle, they weren't allowed to drive it because the rental car wasn't under their name. Things didn't soon get better for the pair. Only after a few hours were they allowed to get everything out of the rental car. The impound would not allow them to drive the car out of the lot, making their chances of getting to the rodeo seem even bleaker.

Both friends began to frantically make phone calls from inside a nearby motel to other fellow riders on the circuit. The only way to salvage the trip would be to have another competitor fill in for them during one of their events. Everybody had already arrived at Waco two days prior and had been in full swing. Their only hope was to use the PRCA tracer system, an online database to track where and when events would take place. Competitors' names would come up on the list and you could get their names and contact information with the hope of reaching out to them. If a competitor had signed up for an event, they could swap with another rider so as to be able to compete on a different day.

At this rate, the only way Tre and Chris would still be eligible to compete would be to swap with riders over the weekend. Their hope was to find riders who were located east of them who could pick them up and head west to Waco together. After a few hours of dialing numbers and coming up empty, they came to the conclusion that they had missed out on the opportunity. Every rider was already east of them and competing. They had no choice but to head home on a flight.

After hitching a ride to the airport from a generous couple they had met in their motel lobby the previous night, Tre and Chris were on a flight on their way back to Marysville. They were dejected and felt like they had let themselves and the community that had supported them down. On top of their emotional pain, the rental car ended up costing a total of $3,800 to release from the impound, forcing both friends to empty out their savings accounts. The cost put another dent in Tre's plans to buy a car or horses.

As the plane touched down in Sacramento, Tre began to feel uneasy about coming back to the ranch so early. The Flying U ranch was dead quiet when Tre and Chris arrived early in the morning. The fog had continued to linger while sunlight shone brightly through it. In a few hours everyone would be awake and the peaceful calm would be replaced by a cacophony of farm animals and sounds. Branding season was in a couple months, and soon the ranch would be filled with thousands of cattle.

Arriving back at the Flying U without even competing was not the triumphant return that Tre and Chris had envisioned. Just a week earlier both had been in high spirits. But now everything had changed. They would have to explain how and why they weren't able to compete over the weekend. It was hard to admit defeat in this way, a forfeit simply because they couldn't stay away from smoking weed. Rodeo results were available online and tended to be posted an hour after each competition. Only the top qualifiers from each event would have their times posted on the website. Those who were disqualified by getting bucked off a horse or for doing an illegal maneuver were omitted from the results.

As each day passed during the circuit finals, both Tre and Chris received text messages from friends and fellow riders asking where they were. Both were having winning seasons and it was hard for people to believe that they had been bucked off their horses, disqualifying them from the competition.

The feeling of shame continued throughout the weekend as each text came in. Their pride was hurt and so were their pockets.

A LOT HAD happened since that night Tre spent in a Texas jail more than four years earlier. He had since become one of the best black rodeo competitors in the United States. He had had a child, a boy named Logan, with a woman from Compton. There were more wrinkles on his dark brown face and his body had more tattoos that served as reminders of the past and future. When the mother of his child was pregnant, he had been working on the ranch in Marysville, but after the birth of his son, Tre decided it was best to stay closer, so he moved back to Compton with his family. His time at home was split between competing in rodeos, caring for his newborn child, and working odd jobs to make extra money in the off-season.

Living back in his grandmother's home on the eastside of Compton was both a blessing and a curse. On one hand, he was back in the neighborhood that had raised him. The familiarity of his block and the love and support of his friends and family were a departure from the solitary life that he had lived while competing around the United States or working in Northern California. The eldest of five siblings didn't take the responsibility lightly. When he was home, he tried to instill the values that he learned while being away from home—hard work, perseverance, courage, and faith. He tried to teach his siblings that there was a world outside of Compton that was beautiful and expansive.

Being back home also brought him in contact again with the

Spook Town Crips, one of the largest gangs on the eastside of Compton. Like most Crip gangs in Compton, the Spook Town Crips relied on recruiting members from in and around their neighborhood. Being a member of the gang was a foregone conclusion for Tre. Because of his family's involvement, he never had to be initiated into the gang—he was born into it.

His uncles, Woody and Grouch, and his cousins, Antwan and T.R., roamed the streets and often took him along with them. The gang ended up being one of the most powerful educations Tre received. It's where he learned how to read people's body language and identify a threat. Or how to spot an undercover cop by the type of shoes they were wearing. The street code—a system of values guided by respect and loyalty—that his family taught him was never part of any curriculum that he learned in school. This education was only available in Spook Town.

Now, as an adult, the birth of his son, Logan, was transformative. It made Tre work harder than he had ever worked before. Waking up each morning came with a different set of pressures. Before Logan was born, not winning a rodeo meant that Tre would have to pick up an odd job in Compton to make ends meet. After Logan's birth, he had no choice. He *had* to win, to support his family without relying on the gang life that had dominated his early years.

At the same time, the group of friends that he had grown up riding with, Randy, Keenan, Anthony, Kenneth, and others, had officially come together as the Compton Cowboys. Like them, Tre felt the weight of being a black cowboy in a city that was more known for black death than it was for black horse riders. As the youngest and best-known rodeo competitor from the group, Tre was also the most fearless. He lived the way he rode, daring and undaunted. People around Compton knew him by the championship belt buckle that he wore everywhere he went.

One day while on the ranch he was surprised by the appearance of two new horses sent by a friend he had made while working in Texas. The horses brought with them new hope for the future. Things were looking up for the youngest cowboy.

THE DECISION

THE CARS CONTINUED TO WHIP past Keenan and Terrance as both of their horses trotted north on Wilmington Avenue in the midday sun. Since making a right onto the busy boulevard, they had shortened their jovial conversation and shifted their body language.

In a matter of moments, Keenan's five-foot-seven-inch frame had gone from slightly slouched to fully erect, focusing his gaze on each car that zipped past them. As the lead rider, it was Terrance's responsibility to make sure that the road was clear ahead. Keenan would have his eye on their rear.

It had been a few months since Sonny had bolted on Wilmington. That incident had become a running joke in the cowboys' group text chat, but it was far from funny for Keenan, who continued to have nightmares about the experience.

For Terrance, who was almost five years older than Keenan, riding on Wilmington came with even more risks. Terrance had been in the neighborhood longer and had a bigger reputation among the Nutty Blocc Crips. He had been on several of their hit lists for the damage he had done to their gang before he joined the cowboys. His slender face and six-foot-six frame were even harder to miss on a horse.

As they continued to trot, Sonny sensed Keenan's nervousness and began to jump at every passing car.

"Easy, Sonny," he whispered in his ear. "I'm just as scared as you are."

A minute later a black car with dark-tinted windows slowed down next to the two friends and stopped in the middle of the street. As the car's windows rolled down, Keenan and Terrance looked at one another and communicated in an unspoken language. Their first impulse was to immediately let the reins go and gallop away toward safety. Horses could reach speeds of up to thirty miles per hour in a matter of seconds.

Or they could take their chances and stay.

Terrance and Keenan turned their horses in the direction of the ranch in case they had to make a quick escape. But as the tinted glass fell, it was a black woman in her early forties who met their gaze. She was alone in her car. Both of them eased back and their blood pressure returned to normal.

"I love y'all so much! I love me some black cowboys!" she shouted from inside her black Mazda sedan, within which a pair of fuzzy black dice swung from the rearview mirror.

The two looked at each other and chuckled. Crazy lady, they thought, and continued to ride back toward the ranch.

"We love you, too," Terrance shouted as they rode away.

TRE SAT IN the living room later that same day watching a daytime courtroom television show featuring a family locked in a civil dispute over the death of a parakeet.

He had been aimlessly scrolling on his phone for the past thirty minutes at his brother's home in Lynwood, waiting for Logan's mother to call him. It had been over an hour and he began to worry about her whereabouts. He hadn't seen his child in over two months, and the last time something like this happened, she had fled the state with their son. Their relationship had never recovered.

Tre had mixed feelings about being back in Compton. On one hand, it gave him the chance to be around his child again and the rest of the cowboys. But it also deprived him of being able to work on the Flying U ranch and compete in the rodeo circuit full-time. Some days were easier than others. Though he had ambitions of competing again, his leg wasn't fully healed from the fight with Charles and Rambo. Doctors had advised him to stay off it for at least another three months.

In the meantime, he spent hours watching old footage of himself competing in bareback riding competitions, studying his posture and handling of the horse in the same way professional football players studied footage of their opponents before a big game. On the side of the television, near the old record player, were other DVDs of past competitions that he watched from time to time, but it was nowhere near as big as the stack he had at his grandmother's home. Tre was a student of the sport, and even though he wasn't physically fit to ride, being at home had given him the chance to watch his old footage and learn from his mistakes.

As the courtroom drama came to an end, the verdict flashed across the screen: the daughter's parents were found guilty and would have to pay for emotional damages caused as a result of the parakeet's death. Tre smiled and continued to scroll through his phone. Suddenly, his father's name showed up on the screen.

"Hello?"

"Get to the 'hood right now," Tre's father said. His deep baritone voice echoed through Tre's ears. "Something just happened to Marcus. He got shot."

Before Tre had a chance to react to the news about his cousin, Tre's mother's door swung open across the room.

"Did y'all hear about Marcus?" she said. "Greg just called me and said he's at the burger stand where Marcus got killed."

Tre hung up the phone and sank deep into the couch. His body collapsed. He felt the weight of the world and none of it at the same time. Marcus had been like a big brother. Tre had always followed closely in his footsteps, and they were inseparable every time Marcus was out of prison.

Tre hobbled out of the house, still nursing his injured leg, and jumped into his brother's car. They headed to Spook Town. When they pulled up to Cypress Street ten minutes later, the entire neighborhood was blocked off by yellow tape and a police barricade. Police cars and a paramedic van were assembled around the scene, their flashing red and blue lights barely visible in the daytime sun.

"That's my cousin over there!" Tre yelled as the police officers refused to let him past the yellow tape. He continued to yell as two officers denied him access to the crime scene. His cousin Daneisha had joined him. Tre looked at his brother and, without saying a word, knew they needed to find a way around the police line. They both got back in the car and drove around the corner, parking several houses down. With the help of his brother, Tre managed to climb over two fences and traverse two lawns, finally getting to the scene of the crime through the back parking lot of Tony's Burgers.

Marcus's body lay on the ground covered by a white sheet in front of a group of palm trees near the restaurant. There were small orange cones around his body, and five police officers. Some of the Spook Town Crips had also found a way around the barricade and were at the scene, alarming some of the police officers, who were afraid of immediate retaliation. A few of the Spook Town Crips wore blue bandanas on their faces, exposing only their eyes, knowing that the police often used murder scenes to photograph and bust suspected gang members. At this point, the entire neighborhood had gathered around the murder scene to honor Marcus's death.

Marcus had been out of prison for six months on the day he was murdered, August 3, 2018. After two years in prison, his demeanor had changed. He trusted people less and confided only in a small circle of intimate friends and family. He was supposed to be at work the day he was gunned down, but instead he had called off to attend a friend's birthday dinner that evening. While he was washing his car in front of his home, two men approached him, and after a verbal exchange, one of the men fired on Marcus and hit him in the abdomen. Wounded, he ran around the corner to Willowbrook, where he was shot again and eventually passed out in the parking lot of Tony's Burgers, across the street from Bunny's Liquor. He died minutes later on the only patch of green grass near the parking lot.

Word on the street was that his murderers had been on a mission to exact revenge on a group of Spook Town Crips in a quarrel completely unrelated to Marcus. Marcus, however, happened to be in the wrong place at the wrong time. If he had run into his house after being shot the first time, he would still have been alive, but he chose to protect his grandparents from the shooters following him, and so was shot a second time.

Marcus's death almost forced Tre to give up riding. It was these types of assaults—random, spontaneous, and personal—that made kids in the 'hood want to join gangs just to avenge the death of their loved ones. In moments like this, Tre couldn't help but feel that tug of revenge. But throwing his rodeo dreams away also meant that Marcus's son, now left behind, would be without a male figure in his life. With Marcus's death, Tre knew he needed to step it up, and so he assumed the responsibility of helping to raise his cousin's son. He wasn't going to let the streets take the boy's life like they had done to Marcus.

WORD OF MARCUS'S death spread fast throughout the farms. When Keenan first heard, he thought about his own friends and relatives who had passed.

As a child, Keenan knew death intimately; it was a frequent visitor that often showed up unannounced. By thirteen he was numb to the sounds of wailing mothers who hugged the bodies of their lifeless children on the street. His eyes grew accustomed to the vivid night rainbows that the paramedic lights created on the sides of homes—their colors, ironically, matched the blue and red tones that people in the neighborhood were living and dying for.

Anthony experienced the same thing when he became a teenager. Terrance remembered it as a gradual process. Randy went through it, and so did Keiara. Each of their bodies began to store death and trauma the way soldiers who fought in distant lands did, as posttraumatic stress.

These battlefields, however, were in Compton.

Some of their pain was internalized and locked away deep within their cells, only to surface years later in the middle of the night as screams and cold sweats. They hardened their bodies up and formed walls to fortify the space between their skin and the outside world—a tactic rooted in preservation and survival.

Keiara remembers her first night terror following her brother's murder, the screams and the uncontrollable crying and the fits of rage that she unleashed on those closest to her. She didn't understand her pain at the time. But growing up in Compton came with two choices: you toughened up or you became a victim. Being vulnerable was never an option. The vulnerable did not survive.

The biggest issue for each of the cowboys was learning how to incorporate the therapy and healing that the horses provided into their lives. Where horses were the physical cure that brought the cowboys together on the farms, their shared experiences of violence and trauma were the glue that bound them together, whether or not they wanted to admit it.

Randy often thought about Eugene, the young boy who admired the group and accompanied them in the parade. He was part of a different generation, but the times hadn't changed so much that the kid wouldn't face the same problems—he already did, in fact. The posttraumatic stress had started for Randy when he was Eugene's age, but it wasn't until his adult years that he had perspective on that trauma. And that numbness, he felt, was the most dangerous part—when submerged in the violence around you, it becomes normalized, and you don't see how you're affected by it.

While the pain of loss and violence was almost unbearable, horses were often the answer to years of undiagnosed trauma. The horses allowed them to heal and to cope. The everyday routine of taking care of the animals gave them a sense of purpose. Randy recognized how lucky they were to have the horses and the ranch; it was an outlet and a form of therapy that most kids growing up in gang territories did not have. He believed that equine therapy continued to help him and his friends heal, and more so, he believed that the horses healed from their own traumatic pasts as well. It was a give-and-take relationship. Most of their horses had experienced various forms of suffering. Some of them had had abusive owners, while others came from chaotic and harmful environments.

The trauma the cowboys experienced brought them closer to understanding the damaged horses they cared for. It created a symbiosis of love and care that continued to pave a pathway forward. Ultimately, it came down to trust. Randy felt that horses, like humans, were naturally gentle creatures, and, like us, if you nurtured them and fostered peace, you would find it too. And if you didn't? As Keenan would often say, "It's life or death, nigga."

PASSING THE REINS

ANTHONY SOFTLY UNLOCKED THE THREE deadbolts in his front door while his son, Anthony Jr., lay asleep on the couch.

It was an unseasonably cold morning for the month of August. A mysterious cold front had come the night before and the grass outside his home was partially frosted over. Every streetlight was still on in the Imperial Courts projects.

Anthony saw a group of young men in the distance coming home from a party. They reminded him of himself fifteen years ago. At thirty-six, however, he had different objectives. He was a family man and waking up to work at the ranch early each morning was the only thing he cared about these days. After warming up his truck for ten minutes, he stepped outside to place a pair of large orange traffic cones in his parking spot. Assigned parking wasn't allowed in the projects, but nobody dared touch Anthony's cones.

He wiped his side mirror with the outside of his shirt, rearranged the durag that he wore under his beanie, and drove in the direction of the ranch. After making a quick right on Imperial Highway, he made a left on Wilmington just under the freeway overpass and headed south.

Anthony had kept the same morning routine since he first started working at the ranch seven years earlier. This morning's drive was the same as the others: quiet and contemplative. Outside of his time with the animals at the ranch, driving was one of the only times that allowed him to be silent. The ten minutes in the truck gave him the chance to think about the duties he had to complete on the ranch that day. It also was time for his first 'wood of the day and the taste of medically prescribed indica cannabis. Anthony had smoked since he was a teenager as a way to fit in with the older guys in his neighborhood. But as an adult it became a medicinal part of a regime that kept him calm and levelheaded the rest of the day.

The streets were relatively calm as he drove on Wilmington Avenue. Except for the sound of his rumbling truck, a few homeless men, and a pair of sex workers near the corner of Rosecrans, the streets were desolate, almost postapocalyptic. But in just a few hours they would be teaming with black and brown faces on their way to work or school.

Anthony arrived at the ranch minutes before 5 a.m., put his truck in park, and turned off the engine. He looked to his left, hoping to see the car of one of Carlton's girlfriends, but no one was parked there this morning. He waited for a few minutes in his truck while finishing the last part of his blunt and scrolled through his Instagram, catching up on messages he hadn't responded to from the previous night. The idea that Instagram could allow him to see what other people were doing around the world astounded him as he swiped through people's stories and posts. To Anthony, who had hardly ever traveled outside of Compton, it was crazy that he could be on the ranch and simultaneously speaking to people all over the world.

Anthony had always worked with his hands. His father, a retired mechanic, had taught him that manual labor was as close to God's work as one could get. Picking up large barrels of hay to feed the horses and shoveling their droppings was not easy, but he completed these tasks with satisfaction. After all, the ranch had to be in top shape when the kids' program began again early next year. While the ranch relied entirely on donations and grants from donors, it also needed a vibrant youth program. The money that previous donors had left was running out, and if things didn't change soon, Anthony would be out of a job.

At the end of January, there was still no sign of the children that Randy had promised. Anthony's mornings continued as they had been, but something about the ranch felt different. He now had two extra horses to look after. The two new mares from Texas had been given to Tre by a fellow rider, taking up two more stalls, bringing them to almost full capacity. The only thing missing from the ranch now was the sounds of children cleaning the stalls and riding horses for the first time.

But the children never showed. At thirty-six, as the eldest member of the cowboys, it was Anthony's dream to give back to the ranch that had saved his life and to keep it running for future generations. He worried that some of the younger guys were getting too caught up in the image of the Compton Cowboys, rather than giving back to the community. And the clock was ticking—Mayisha had given them a year to find a way to revive their old programs. With dwindling funds and resources, who knew if that would even be enough time.

After Anthony cleaned the stalls that morning, Mayisha and some of her old friends showed up. Anthony straightened up and waved hello. His white tank top was drenched with sweat and dirty from the trailer that he had been cleaning for the past hour. Mayisha was a rare sight at the ranch these days after she had moved. She had only been back to handle financial matters, and she almost never came alone. She was usually accompanied by old friends and people who had volunteered on the ranch throughout the years. Today was no different.

An unknown white woman and man accompanied her assistant,

Kathy, a longtime volunteer, to the horse stalls. They carried clipboards with them and documents, inspecting some of the horses. Anthony took a break from cleaning the trailer to see the transaction. It wasn't the first time Mayisha had sold horses or ranch equipment. When money was low, a horse would go. Sometimes two. Other times it would be a trailer. Every time Mayisha and her friends showed up to the ranch something went missing. This time, one of the trailers that had been used to transport horses over the years was up for sale.

The ranch was slowly becoming a shadow of what it once was as Mayisha's retirement party drew closer and closer. As things disappeared, questions about the fate of the ranch began to grow within the cowboys' circle.

Keenan had arrived at the ranch minutes after the group showed up. "What's up, man?" he said to Anthony, who continued to watch the group, who were now in Sonny's stall, inspecting him for what they believed could be an eventual sale.

"You know Mayisha wants to sell the horses?" Anthony said to him. They both leaned on the gate, watching the transaction take place before their eyes. "Kathy told me they want to sell Sonny. You better buy him before they can do that."

Keenan's body tensed up. Selling Sonny would mean losing another horse in his life.

"Oh, hell no," he responded. "Shit, I already talked to her about buying him a while ago, so I don't know what they're doing over there."

"It feels like they don't want to see us win," Anthony said, puffing on a cigarette.

Tensions on the ranch were escalating between the old guard and the new generation. More and more of the elder Compton Junior Posse volunteers were now part of the transition team, and it was their job to ensure that nothing was left behind. They wanted to sell as many things as possible, even including May- isha's home.

The cowboys, on the other hand, had different plans.

"I already bought Kota a few months ago," Anthony said. "I suggest you do the same for Sonny."

Keenan nodded his head and agreed.

THE PARTY

THE EVENT PLANNERS ARRIVED AT the ranch much earlier than expected on the morning of Mayisha's retirement party. The tent now covered the entire arena, creating a large shaded area for people to sit. Three hundred invitations had gone out weeks before, and nearly two hundred people had RSVP'd. The neighborhood hadn't seen this many people on Caldwell Street since the last of the Akrite parties when the cowboys were teenagers. Valet parking attendants began to arrive at 10 a.m. that morning to set up for the day. Mayisha worried that the city would get involved if they caused a traffic jam, so the ranch rented out parking on someone's abandoned lot.

Inside the ranch, the smell of delicious Jamaican food and smoky barbecue filled the air, while a large black grill blew hot steam out from its sides. Slowly, more people began to show up. The donors who had followed Mayisha's vision of providing children from Compton with horses were all in attendance. Their hair had greyed over the years and some of them needed help walking, supported by canes and their own memories of their experiences on the ranch over the years.

Like Mayisha, they, too, were there to announce that they would no longer be a part of the ranch's operations.

Teal and yellow design ribbons adorned each of the tables, with sets of flowers that matched the color scheme. On a typical day, the ranch embodied an image of toughness that was in stark contrast to the pretty decorations of the event. The red carpet that led to the tent made the space feel like a spectacle rather than a sanctuary for so many members of the community. A bit of the ranch's sacredness was lost.

Randy and the rest of the cowboys wore their best outfits. Their collared shirts were tucked in, their Stetson hats were crisp, and their boots had just been shined. They looked like the images of black cowboys that they had wanted to see as children in their own history books: confident, young, black, and free. Tre, in particular, wore his Bill Pickett championship belt with pride. It shone in the sun and reflected a kaleidoscope of bright blue and gold flashes of light on whoever stood in front of him. Since Marcus's death, Tre had been spending less time on the ranch and wearing his belt less, but that day, he moved with his shoulders back and his head and chin to the sky as he walked on the red carpet and into the shaded tent, eager to boast about how well he had done for himself in the rodeo world since the donors last saw him as a teenager.

Mayisha's contribution was irreplaceable, but with the passing of the ranch operations to Randy, the community now had to rely on him for direction. It was a monumental day. For Randy, it meant that his dream of running the ranch was now coming true. For the community and black cowboy culture in Compton, it meant that western-style riding was back, bringing with it the hope of attracting more at-risk youth who preferred that over the tamer English style. English style had felt like a departure from the history of black cowboys in the West, at times even a departure from blackness.

When the partygoers sat down to eat, an emcee got on the stage and welcomed everyone to the event. She spoke of the impact that Mayisha had on the community and the hole that her exit would be leaving. Mayisha sat near the back of the tent with her husband, Jody, a longtime volunteer, observing the party with the same careful eyes that saw a mound of backyard dirt turn into one of the only black ranches in the West.

Mayisha and Jody were both now well into their sixties and had lived through some of the worst and best times at the ranch. Their fingers and hands held tightly together on top of the table, they remembered their first parade and the looks on people's faces as they proudly rode in unison through Compton. They also remembered the gang wars that extinguished many young black lives in the 1990s. They remembered the dozens of bullets that found a home in some of their riders and those that almost took the lives of others. Those days were the hardest until Jody, a military veteran, had made a decision.

"I put my body on the line for my country," he told Mayisha, remembering the bullets that zipped by his head one night during one of the gang wars. "Why shouldn't I do the same thing for my community?" He watched and quietly ate the food in front of him, thinking about the things he had seen over the years, preferring to not be around so many people.

The words that were shared that afternoon by the speakers spoke of a glorious past, one filled with great challenges and rewarding outcomes. It was supposed to be a party, but it felt like a celebration of a bygone era—ceremonial in the way a wake or funeral party often is.

The future of the ranch was uncertain and everyone in attendance looked at the cowboys for answers that they did not have. Speaking about the future felt taboo, and until Randy stepped onstage, not a word was said about it.

Randy hopped onto the stage and kissed his aunt on the cheek, complimenting her on her yellow West African kente cloth dress.

A wide electric smile showed nearly every single tooth in his mouth.

"I'm so proud of my aunt," he said, smiling to the crowd. "I'm so proud to be able to continue her legacy. Most importantly, I'm proud to be a cowboy."

He spoke of the journey that he had embarked on as a child and the process by which they had arrived at this moment.

"We're in the process of developing five different programs for the ranch," he said, while members in the audience clapped cautiously, skeptical of his plans. "It's going to be called the Compton Junior Equestrian and will include skills training and clinical therapy for our youth. We want to see this work in Compton and then use it as a model for other 'hoods in the U.S. and around the world."

After the party ended, Randy congregated with some donors whom he had known since he was a child. They congratulated him and were eager to hear about his plans in greater detail. The idea to replicate the ranch model was something Mayisha never spoke about. Her mission was to save Compton's youth, but Randy had more far-reaching dreams.

"I'm trying to get the ranch running smoothly with the hopes of taking this model and applying it in different cities across the U.S.," he said while adjusting his belt buckle. "We're connected to black cowboys in Philadelphia, cowboys in Chicago, and also with cowboys overseas. We just need the resources to do this in a big way and put ranches like this one in inner-city environments where there's a lack of nature, because we see that this model works."

A group of four white donors looked at Randy with speculative eyes. Here was a young man with big dreams but with no proven track record. The model would be hard to accomplish, but before he could expand he would first have to find a way to keep his ranch alive.

"What makes you so confident that this model would work somewhere else?" an elderly woman in a blue dress asked.

"Because we believe in the horses and their ability to make everything better. They changed us, and we think they can have the same effect on at-risk youth everywhere."

THE GOLDEN FLASK

THE SOUND OF A POLICE helicopter buzzed over Kenneth's home as he tossed and turned uncontrollably under the soft satin sheets. It had been three days since he last took a sip of alcohol, and his body was beginning to pay the price for it.

The lack of alcohol in his system had thrown off his senses of hearing and touch. Every sound in his home was painfully amplified. The kitchen faucet, leaking from years of overuse, dripped loudly into an overflowing cooking pan. Its sound echoed throughout the house. Outside his bedroom window, two raccoons scoured inside a trash can for food, while Ebony's frequent neighs and the sound of Kenneth's own pulsating heart created a symphonic measure that only he and the animals around him could detect. Every drop of cold sweat that his body released felt like the purging of collected evils that had haunted him and other members of the Atkins family for decades.

The night sweats were the most haunting. In his nightmares, Kenneth saw vivid images of his paternal great-grandparents, their arms stretched out to him, attempting to save him from the path of self-destruction that alcohol had once brought them to. He was simultaneously transported back to his childhood, where he saw a younger version of himself, a boy with skinny arms and short-cropped hair, riding a horse in an empty, foggy riding arena. He saw a boy who was dying to be loved but also born to be hated.

He spent the next day glued to his couch, his naked body

covered only by two large blankets. This cold turkey process required isolation, so only his mother stayed around to see it. Like other women in the Atkins family, it wasn't her first time seeing a man she loved go through detox. Almost thirty years before, her husband had battled the same addiction. He, too, had stopped drinking after it began to drastically affect their marriage and the safety of their home. Seeing her son go through the same experience decades later was hard to watch, but she knew that there was no other way.

The devil had attempted to take her husband before, and the devil had come calling for her son.

Kenneth didn't eat for three days. His body became too weak to perform even the most basic things, like using the restroom or brushing his teeth. On the fourth day, the pungent smell of week-old sweat and vomit began to seep through the living room couch. At night, his ancestors once again stood by his bed.

As he continued to cough out mucus and blood, images of different relatives continued to flash before his eyes. Some of the faces he saw weren't warm. They were sinister, and they were dark. These were the faces of men in his family whose drinking had completely destroyed their families. These men were the descendants of freed slaves from the South who had migrated to the Midwest to embark on a new life, only to be denied the promise of freedom. They were men who found freedom in the comfort of glass bottles.

Their hardened eyes pierced his skin, each stare urging him to drink again and again, assuring him that alcohol was the only thing that would keep him alive.

During the sixth night, when there was no indication that his symptoms would ever go away, the first sets of ancestors returned to his bed accompanied by what he remembered as the presence of God. Their presence felt warm and lit the dark room with bright yellow tones. They had a message and had come back to tell him that he wasn't alone and, most importantly, that he was loved. The night sweats and the shivering ended the next day and his body slowly began to regain consciousness. When he woke up the next morning, he heard the echo of Kendrick Lamar's song "Swimming Pools" in his head.

Kenneth thought about the generations of men in his family who had come before him. The Atkins men were always known for their sternness and quiet disposition. His father had been sober for over twenty-five years, and Kenneth wished he could do the same. It wasn't his first time attempting to quit drinking, but there was something dire about this time. It was his first time seeing his ancestors, and it would be his last.

It took a little over a month for his body to fully adjust. His sleep schedule had normalized and his appetite had returned. He began to wake up at 6 a.m. to feed his animals and clean Ebony's stall. After making himself breakfast and smoking his first 'wood, he drove to his job as an administrator at a residential care facility for elders. Because his parents owned the facility they welcomed him back to work with open arms. After a few hours of checking up on patients and employees, he would drive back to Compton, exercise in a local gym, cook, and then smoke again. Alcohol was now completely out of his life, and for the first time in years, he was able to sustain sobriety. He was off probation and able to drive with a court-appointed breathalyzer in his car that he had to blow into before driving.

Even better, his relationship with the rest of the cowboys improved. While his body was detoxing, the images of horses and his friends drove him to find a clearer purpose. He wanted to help others know of the importance of horses in Compton. He wanted to be seen differently too, for kids to look at him and think about options besides playing basketball or football. To realize that horses were an option too.

The art in Kenneth's living room reminded him of the person he wanted to be. On one wall stood a portrait of a younger Kenneth, with short hair, wearing a helmet, atop a horse preparing to jump. He had the look of someone in the midst of their true calling—those moments when the universe reminds you that you are exactly where you are supposed to be.

His other walls were adorned by horse paintings. In the kitchen were two black horse sculptures that stood proudly in the center of the table. If he were to stay sober this time, it would be almost entirely due to his love for horse riding and his friends. Sixty days of sobriety had passed, and it had been years since he felt this healthy.

Not being able to ride Ebony while going through withdrawal was the hardest part about the process. The thought of being able to ride her again helped him stay the course; it kept his mind occupied and helped him combat his addiction. He wondered about Compton High School and the impact horses could have on teenagers who were also battling alcohol addiction, how horses could bring teenagers back to nature, here, in the middle of the 'hood, and how *empowering* that was. There was nothing more dangerous than a smart black man on a horse.

BACK AT THE RANCH

IT HAD ONLY BEEN A couple of months since Mayisha saw Anthony at her retirement party, but she walked up to him and looked at him like she hadn't seen him in years. Her greyish hair was covered by a turquoise-and-black hat that covered just enough of her face to keep the sun away.

"Hi, Mama," Anthony yelled, running toward Mayisha, while Keenan and Terrance followed closely behind. "Oh . . . youuu look good!" he said, examining her physique the way an old friend would after not seeing their friend for a while. "You put on some weight, Mama! Jody been feeding you good, I see!"

Anthony did another full circle around Mayisha, continuing to laugh hysterically. "You looooooking good."

Mayisha smiled and blushed, her light brown cheeks lighting up in the sun. She glanced down at her tight black pants and red-colored toenails. "Oh yeah, you know," she replied in a soft tone while continuing to laugh. "I'm doing okay."

Since her retirement party, Mayisha rarely came to the ranch. When she did come, to pick up mail, or see her children, she continued to take things back to her home in Riverside County. Some days it would be a horse, others it would be equipment from the ranch. Her home was on the market, and though she had plans to sell the property soon, her one-year lease was coming to an end in Norco, forcing her to rethink her plans.

"Anthony, I need you to do me a favor," Mayisha asked after

the laughter subsided. "Can you bring me six of those grooming kits buckets?"

"Six?" Anthony replied in a sarcastic tone.

"Yeah, I got a buyer," she responded.

Anthony nodded and walked back to the tack room, accompanied by Terrance, to find the grooming kits, leaving Keenan alone with Mayisha in the driveway. The two cast shadows behind them as they walked together toward the back of the ranch, the same as they had done since they were teenagers. Their waist sizes had increased slightly, but their pants still hung loosely on their legs.

As Anthony rummaged through the equipment room, he noticed that its contents were dwindling by the day. Mayisha's plans to help other horse-riding programs in her new neighborhood were evident, but at the current rate there would be no ranch equipment left in the tack room for the Compton Cowboys' own youth program.

Keenan anxiously pointed his toe in the gravel and put his hands inside the pouch of his black Compton Cowboys sweater while they waited for Anthony to return. "You know I'm back now?" he said without making eye contact with Mayisha.

Mayisha looked up at him. "You're back?" she asked, surprised.

"Yeah, the rent was getting too high in Inglewood so we had to move back."

Mayisha looked at him and ruffled through her bag with one of her hands, searching for her phone.

"But we're doing good now," he said, raising his voice. "We're back on it, and making sure things run smoothly around here."

"Mhm," Mayisha responded with the same speculation that a loving mother would have of a child who hadn't yet shown that they'd overcome their bad habits.

The last time she and Randy had spoken, they had disagreed over the day-to-day operations of the ranch and the image that the cowboys were exporting to the outside world. She believed that the cowboys were more interested in self-promotion than they were about giving back to their community. Riding around the neighborhood bareback and in sandals was departing from the values she had fought tirelessly to uphold. Mayisha wasn't yet convinced that they were interested in running the program. She believed that the cowboys' best chance for survival was to continue building the relationships that she had created with wealthy donors.

If they were smart, she thought, they would continue to ride English. It would expose them to a different social class, one with more connections and funding. She believed that the clean-cut, conservative aspects of riding English were what brought respect to her program in the first place. Mayisha wanted that part of her program to continue, but that was the biggest challenge for the cowboys. It was February and only four children had showed up to the first orientation. Perhaps it was Mayisha's initial choice to switch over to English that continued to deter many of Compton's youth. Randy continued to hope that more young riders would show up with the switch back to western, fulfilling his dream of getting back to the roots of black cowboy culture.

COWBOY BEEF

"HEY, YOU FROM THE COMPTON Cowboys?" a voice asked Kenneth while he pulled on two wire cables at the gym.

The unknown man stood a few feet behind him while he finished his set. He asked again, and this time he grabbed Kenneth's shoulder and gestured with his hands to take off his headphones.

The man was in his midforties and had prison tattoos all over his body. His lifted chest and forty-five-degree-angle-pointed feet, one slightly hidden behind the other, signaled that he was from the streets.

"Are you part of the Compton Cowboys?" he asked again. A friend of his had now joined him, standing almost the same way. Both waited for a response.

"Yeah, I am," Kenneth finally responded while he put the weights back down on the floor and took his headphones off. His own shoulders tightened up and his chest bulked in front of him, ready for confrontation.

"I'm from Compton and a member of the Hill riders and my boys and I don't like the way y'all are representing black cowboys," the man said while rubbing his hands together in front of his chest. "Y'all look like some clowns wearing sandals and shit when you ride."

The two men were part of another black horse-riding group on the Hill, a horse ranch located in South Central that had burned down in 2012.

Riders from the Hill were one of the first groups of black urban cowboys in Southern California. Like the ranch on the farms, the Hill became an oasis for black riders in South Central who arrived from the South in the 1960s. Within a matter of years, the Hill had grown into a thriving horse-riding community, and like the ranch, it was a place that gave African-American youth like Tre and Keiara a place to congregate and ride. In 2012, however, the Hill mysteriously burned down late one night. Arson was always suspected; one of the horses had been doused with gasoline and set ablaze, causing the rest of the stables to also catch fire. The fire deeply impacted the lives of many of its riders, causing Keiara and Tre to move their horses to Mayisha's ranch. The others who were left without a place to house their horses were forced to sell.

Kenneth backed up from the two men and braced himself for a fight.

"You think kids in the 'hood are going to respect y'all when y'all are doing that clown shit?" the man asked.

Since the cowboys first officially banded together, they had been criticized for not always wearing traditional cowboy clothing whenever they rode through the streets of Compton. Older generations of riders from the Hill, like the man who stood in front of Kenneth, believed it was disrespectful and portrayed the wrong image of black cowboy culture.

"We don't have to wear tucked-in shirts and baggy jeans with our boots," Kenneth explained. "We have our own style and our own way of doing things."

The conversation continued with no end in sight. The differences in generational views about cowboy culture weren't going to get solved that day, and Kenneth knew he couldn't fight both of them. He knew he would put up a fight, but he needed Randy to be there.

"Hold up, let me call my homie," Kenneth told them. "He'll be able to explain what we're trying to do."

Cowboy beef had become a growing concern in Compton. While the Compton Cowboys came from a Crip neighborhood, riders from the Hill lived in a neighborhood full of Piru Bloods. They were linked by family and gang affiliation, and that didn't end when they mounted their horses.

When Randy arrived, the four walked out to a quiet part of the parking lot, where he and Kenneth prepared for the unexpected.

"I done had people I know die for this Compton horse life," the man said, raising his voice, creating a scene as people walked in and out of the gym. His passion and love for horses was evident as his voice echoed throughout the parking lot. "I'm a real cowboy and we put our hats on and boots and go rope shit, and y'all making us look bad."

The older cowboys' issue stemmed from the media attention that the Compton Cowboys had been receiving over the past year. They felt like the younger men hadn't paid their dues and were riding on the coattails of the legacy established by riders from the Hill. The energy that he brought to the conversation echoed all around the city of Compton. It was rough and raw and intense.

To an outsider, four black men standing in a parking lot facing one another could have resembled a fight about gang territory, women, or drugs. But the conversation was entirely about horses and cowboys. They went back and forth and it became clear that neither side wanted to fight—the elder just wanted to communicate his concern for the future of black cowboys in Compton.

"We just have a different approach," Randy explained to the riders from the Hill. "We're not new to Compton, I'm born and raised in the farms. My whole family is from the farms and my auntie has been doing this since before we were born."

Slowly the man's tense posture eased up. The look in his eyes went from anger to understanding as he continued to take in Randy's words.

"I done buried two of my homies this past year," Randy explained. "We're really about this 'hood and cowboy life."

The conversation deescalated after each person explained their stance. Neither cowboy was right or wrong, and the altercation instead reflected a broader issue that was affecting black cowboys across Los Angeles. Older riders were becoming increasingly disconnected from the younger generation. When older black riders first began riding, they experienced discrimination and rejection. They had to look twice as good and ride three times better than the average white cowboy. It's the reason why black rodeo competitions like the Bill Pickett Invitational Rodeo were started in the first place. The younger generation of riders were bringing their own style and customs to horse riding. They were taking ownership.

The talk opened up a conversation that Randy had been meaning to have with other black riders in and around Compton. The showdown became the perfect opportunity for him to shatter the stereotypes that people had about the Compton Cowboys. The suggestion of organizing a riding event together was raised as a way to unite both groups. Riding together, they believed, would help create better bonds with other riders, and it would help the older generation understand the mission that Randy and his friends were on. Like the riders from the Hill, the Compton Cowboys were on a mission to eradicate stereotypes about black cowboys and reinsert themselves and others back into the history books.

Kenneth, on the other hand, couldn't let the situation go that easily. The two men had rubbed him the wrong way and confirmed that he was one of the most hated cowboys in Compton. His fame and notoriety on social media was becoming a source of jealousy. Other black riders thought he was a joke, and that didn't sit well with him.

"There's Blood and Crip beef in the 'hood, but this is cowboy beef," he said as he drove away from the group in the direction of the ranch.

KEENAN PUFFED ON a cigarette and took a long look around the ranch. There was still a lot of work to do before the guys showed up, and if he hurried he could feed all the horses and clean some of the stalls in the next hour.

He flicked his cigarette butt into the air and continued filling each stall with hay. It had been almost two weeks since he had fully moved back, and the ranch hand life was starting to become routine again. When he was working at a restaurant in downtown Los Angeles, an average weekend commute would take him almost an hour. Now his commute was only steps away.

"You looking good today," he told Sonny, while the horse dove his head deep inside of the hay feeder in his stall. "Eat all the hay you can while it's dry, 'cause the rain might come back later."

Tre's and Mike's backs both rested on Tre's car in the driveway while they both waited for other cowboys to show up. The two wide-shouldered former football players and single fathers had been spending more time together these days. In his free time, Tre had begun cutting hair and had booked an appointment with Keenan.

A young Latina woman in her twenties walked out of the next-door home, causing both friends to look. Even Byron, who was on the porch smoking a Newport, turned her way.

COWBOY BEEF | 201

"Who's that?" Tre asked while touching the side of his freshly cut hair. "She need to be coming over here, you feel me?" Mike hummed and nodded in agreement.

Since the youth program wasn't in full operation yet, weekends on the ranch had been quiet over the past few months. But after Kenneth was approached by riders from the Hill, certain members of the cowboys had different opinions about which action to take, prompting an informal meeting at the ranch that day.

In a surprising turn of events, one of the Hill riders extended an invitation to ride with them in two weeks. The ride would also include other black riding groups from Southern California, and if everyone who was expected to show up did, it would be one of the largest gatherings of black cowboys in recent years.

The invitation was enticing but not enough for Kenneth. He preferred to skip it, arguing instead that the Hill riders "wanted to steal their clout" and try to ride the bandwagon of attention that the cowboys had been receiving since they officially banded together more than two years earlier.

"Them niggas from the Hill aren't from the farms," he said. "They're jealous of us because we can wake up in the morning and ride our horses. Them niggas can't do that and they're mad that they have to leave their homes and drive somewhere to get on horses."

Anthony's and Terrance's opinions aligned more with Kenneth's. As two of the eldest and most connected to the street life, their views were more aggressive.

"We can handle the situation whatever way they want to," Anthony said. "They mad 'cause we're younger than they are, but I can bring the chopper to the ride if necessary."

The threat of gun violence to settle the issues with the Hill cowboys worried Randy. His hope to unite all black cowboys would be shattered if bad blood with the Hill continued. A war between the Hill and the farms would automatically incite a corresponding war between members of the Bloods and Crips.

Mariah appeared as they waited, pushing Lux's grey stroller. The toddler eventually got out and started walking around the group, adorable in his sweater and sweats combination. The more time his son spent with the horses, the happier Randy became. Horses were becoming a big part of Lux's life, and his comfort level with them was increasing rapidly, which assured Randy that the Hook family tradition of horse riding would continue.

As the young parents watched their only son, Tre wrapped a barber's robe around Keenan, who was perched on a makeshift stool. Because the rodeo circuit didn't begin for another three months, Tre was cutting hair to make money. He had learned by doing his own hair and then worked on close friends and family. He didn't charge most of the cowboys and only took whatever they could afford, but cutting hair was now more than a hobby for him. Weeks before cutting Keenan's hair, he had enrolled in barber college, paying the $1,500 enrollment fee with the hope of being officially licensed at the end of the course.

The temperature continued to drop as the sun faded. The guys paced the ranch grounds in order to stay warm, smoking and drinking bottles of beer all the while. Keenan's wife had joined the group and stood next to Mariah while she braided the mane of one of the horses.

When Keiara's black Chevrolet Suburban pulled up to the ranch, the group had already been drinking and smoking for hours. Ever since she moved Penny from the Gardena stables to the ranch weeks before, she had been spending more time with the cowboys, even though her injury continued to hinder her ability to ride.

"What's up, Kiki?" everyone said as she and Taylor walked up to the group.

"Hiiiiiiiii, pretty little girrrrrrrrrrlllllll," Keenan said from the barber chair, pointing at Taylor.

"Taylor, say hi to Keenan," Keiara told Taylor.

At this point in her life, Taylor had been around horses as much as she had been around humans. She waved at the group and immediately walked back to the stables, searching for Penny.

The altercation with the Hill cowboys was a bit more complicated for Tre and Keiara than it was for the rest of the cowboys. Both had first learned how to ride on the Hill and were still connected to the riders. Though the Hill was only a shadow of what it once had been since its stables had burned, for Keiara the place reminded her of the days she had spent there when her brother was still alive. But like the rest of the cowboys, she had mixed views about the new generation of riders who claimed to be from the Hill.

"I don't know a lot of the new riders over there," she said while putting a pair of riding pads on Penny's back. "I only know the older riders, and it seems like a lot of the younger niggas are on some new shit that I don't really fuck with. One time when I was a kid, me and my brother and some other homies jumped one of them in one of the stables," she added while securing a bridle on her horse.

That the Hill was going through its own transformation wasn't the cause of concern for the group. They, too, were in the process of creating a new vision for black cowboys. The deeper issue lay in the image that the Compton Cowboys were creating for themselves. Word from the black riding community had said that several other black cowboy groups throughout California had issues with the way that the Compton Cowboys were promoting themselves. Not having the support of their fellow black cowboys would undermine the success and image the Compton Cowboys were trying to create.

"I would love to be unified with other black cowboys," Randy said to the group, his black cap and black Ray-Ban sunglasses concealing his eyes and most of his face. "But the Willie Lynch theory is a real thing in the 'hood. Black people always finding ways to hate against one another. It's too common. We try to knock each other down. If we show up to the ride and there's beef with them, then that's just that Willie Lynch shit happening."

The idea that black cowboys could quarrel, according to Randy, derived from a speech given by a slave owner named Willie Lynch in the early 1700s. The speech detailed a "secret" the master had found—that is, separating enslaved Africans from one another would pit the divided groups against each other. The theory resonated with the Cowboys.

"We're just different than them niggas," Kenneth said while sitting as far away from the alcohol as possible. "We ain't gotta wear cowboy boots all the time and—"

Randy immediately interjected, interrupting Kenneth's views, "Yeah, we're different, but there's a movement that we're trying to create with them as well. And things like Instagram have helped us promote that culture. The goal has always been for every black cowboy to come out of the shadows. Black cowboys have been around for years but they haven't had the energy that we have, and we're trying to break all the fucking barriers."

Everyone nodded in agreement.

"Definitely," Keenan said, checking out his hair in a small mirror that Tre had put in front of him.

Kenneth was the only one who didn't nod, still visibly upset by his confrontation with the Hill riders.

In spite of the issues that were being addressed that day, the mood of the ranch had shifted. Kenneth's past actions might have given his friends a reason to isolate him even further from the group, but the exact opposite had happened: it brought them closer together. The rest of the cowboys felt attacked and saw Kenneth as one of their own and were willing to protect him.

The pressures of keeping the ranch alive and the reality that young people weren't showing up in ways that they had hoped for were concealed by the beers and laughs. At one point, Randy went to the back shed and brought out two boards with older photos of the cowboys when they were members of the Compton Junior Posse. It was something that he liked to do whenever the cowboys got together, to remind everyone where they had come from. Each photo on the board told a different story. It reminded the cowboys of the bond they had shared since they were children.

Everyone gathered around it.

"There goes Slim," Carlton pointed out while holding Lux in his arms. "And his mama, too." Since Slim had passed away months ago, photos and memories were all they had of the brother they had lost. Another photo showed Randy on his childhood horse, named Lookattime, a white Arabian that was donated to the ranch by the University of Southern California's spirit squad.

Their young faces and bright blue shirts stood out in every photo, prompting Keenan to yell out "Blue Lives Matter" from his stool, causing everyone to laugh.

"Blue lives fucking matter, y'all," Keenan said sarcastically.

A photo of Mariah and Randy sitting on a fence at the ranch brought back memories of the past fifteen years that they had shared together. The birth of Lux had brought them back together, but also introduced new challenges.

Keenan took off his robe, stepped off the stool, and crouched down to look at the photos of their youth.

"Damn, you were a chicken head," he said to Mariah, who was wearing a red hooded sweater to cover her hair in the photo. "I remember that day," he continued. "That's when you and Randy first met."

"Me? A chicken head? Nigga, your horses are some chicken heads," she said, making the entire group roar with laughter. She looked directly at Keenan, who didn't have a response.

Randy quickly responded in defense of Keenan and the horses. "Yeah, okay, maybe, but how we got one of the top hairstylists in the game that lives on the ranch? And these horses can't get no love? It doesn't make no sense!"

Though some of the tension had eased, Randy decided it was best not to ride with the Hill riders. It was too soon, and Anthony and Kenneth were still on edge following the altercation. On top of the reluctance to ride and make peace with the other black cowboys, the rains had made many of the trails and streets unsafe to ride in. All the cowboys could do was hope that things would cool off on their own. At the end of the day, it was what was best for both the community and for the future of black riders in Compton.

BUNNY'S LIQUOR OR SWIMMING POOLS

KENNETH SAT ON HIS COUCH and watched television as the rain continued to fall outside. A flash flood warning blinked across his cell phone. It had been sporadically raining on the farms all week, limiting the activities that he could do to stay busy. Going to the gym would require leaving his house, and going to work would require driving even farther away. While he was surrounded by his animals, the rain only increased the loneliness that burned inside him.

Earlier in the week, when he woke up to the sound of rain, he looked outside his window and saw grey skies. It immediately triggered depressive thoughts and anxiety. The voices that he hadn't heard in months had returned and were urging him to drink.

"Go get some. A little bit won't hurt," one voice said from deep inside his body.

When the voices got louder and louder he couldn't take the torment anymore and mounted Ebony and rode to Bunny's Liquor, across the street from where Marcus was murdered, where candles still remained on the patch of grass where he took his last breaths. On his way out of Bunny's, he stopped by the makeshift memorial, opened the bottle, and poured out some cognac in honor of his late friend, then poured some down his throat.

"RIP, big homie," he said while still mounted on Ebony.

The following three days were a blur. On Wednesday he made three trips to Bunny's, and by the time Thursday had arrived, he had made a total of ten. He drank directly from the bottle until there was none left, making up for months of sobriety. Every trip to Bunny's was blurrier than the one before, as he slipped in and out of consciousness and drank until the voices in his head were drowned out.

Empty bottles of cognac lay on his kitchen counter while he continued to watch television that morning. To the left of the television was a framed photo of a younger Kenneth, who had yet to try alcohol. He was young and he still looked hopeful.

Drinking had sparked a dangerous cycle in Kenneth's life. Every time he drove he had to take a breathalyzer test in his car. If there was a trace of alcohol on his breath it wouldn't allow the car to start, which forced him to ride Ebony instead. But when it rained it was too slippery to ride, which left him with limited options.

Kenneth had fallen back into the vicious cycle that he had been through for years.

Keenan and Anthony were fixing an old refrigerator on the ranch, two days after Kenneth had relapsed, when he appeared through the driveway mounted on Ebony.

"What the fuck y'all doing?" he yelled for both of them to hear. "Y'all having a garage sale or something?"

Anthony and Keenan looked at one another and suspected the same thing. Kenneth's speech was hurried and his energy was higher than usual, clear signs that he had been drinking.

Keenan walked up to him and shook his hand, smelling a whiff of alcohol on his breath, confirming his suspicion. Kenneth's triggers also involved some of his closest friends. Every time

Charles joked about his drinking problem it sent Kenneth spiral-ing into self-loathing. Weeks before his relapse, Charles had sent him a video of an Alcoholics Anonymous ad that he had seen on the side of the road. He sent the video as a joke, but it had the opposite effect. Shame made it harder to fight the temptation.

The morning after Kenneth rode into the ranch with alcohol on his breath, Randy and Keenan invited him for breakfast at Spires, a family restaurant blocks away from the farms. After or-dering, Kenneth wanted to let Randy know what he had already suspected.

He spoke in a soft tone while he ate his eggs and bacon, re-sorting back to a childlike version of himself when he felt like he had news to share that would disappoint his parents.

"I just wanted to let you know that I relapsed this week," he said in a soft tone while he slowly chewed on his food. "Not drinking felt like torture, and I know you probably already knew, but I just wanted to tell you."

Randy took a drink of his coffee and nodded his head. Keenan did the same.

"I could tell," Randy said. "I had a feeling it was going to hap-pen. I just didn't know when."

The three friends continued to eat their food.

"You have to know your limits, man, and find some balance. We love you and we're always going to look out for you, but you're an adult. We're not going to police you, but you have to be more responsible."

"Exactly," Keenan said, nodding in agreement. "You have to do what's best for you."

"I don't know how to find that balance, though," Kenneth said urgently, raising his voice. "I feel like I'm always running from it and alcohol is everywhere I turn. I feel like I can't have fun with y'all because there's always alcohol involved. When I'm not drinking I'm miserable, and when I'm drinking I'm also losing because I'm potentially going to do some stupid shit."

"You become someone else when you drink and you talk about doing shit like killing people," Randy said. "Then when you come down from it you get really bad shakes and withdrawals. Once you start you just can't stop," he continued.

Kenneth looked down at his food again. He was quiet and reflective.

"I want to fight it but I don't know what to do," he finally said. "I don't know what to do."

IT HAD BEEN only a few days since Kenneth relapsed, and conversations about his health began to resurface between the cowboys. "I don't think he's going to make it this time," Anthony said while cleaning out a stall on Friday morning. "It was just a matter of time before he started drinking again." Other members of the cowboys felt the same.

The next day brought its share of new concerns for the ranch. It had rained heavily throughout the week and many of the stalls were sloppy with mud—the perfect conditions for thrush. On Saturday, after the rain had cleared up and a cold gust of easterly winds arrived, Pirate, an older Thoroughbred, began limping around the arena. The ranch's oldest and most beloved horse was favoring his back left leg, walking slowly while dragging his left leg in the mud. His leg was swollen to almost twice the size of his right. Keenan woke up that morning to check on the horses and immediately called Randy. Calling a veterinarian would cost just as much as calling someone to put Pirate down, and either option would force him to dig deeper into a pot of resources that continued to dwindle as each day passed.

After an hour of deliberation Randy decided it was best to call the ranch veterinarian, Fabio, a Mexican man in his fifties who had been associated with the ranch for years. He was kind and soft-spoken, with a heavy accent. He spoke with his hands when he could no longer come up with the right words to describe something.

"Did you see what happened to horse?" he asked Keenan upon his arrival, gesturing in the direction of the arena. "Did horse fight with other horse?"

"I don't know if they fought, all I know is that I woke up this morning and Pirate was limping," Keenan said. "That's all I know."

Fabio asked Keenan to help him pull Pirate into the middle of the arena for a deeper inspection. Charles, Carlton, and Randy looked on while Pirate hobbled to the center of the arena.

"Damn, man, Pirate really in some pain, boy," Charles said out loud while he rubbed the sides of his shoulders. The temperature had dropped significantly.

"Yeah, man," Randy replied. "I don't know what Fabio's going to say, but we'll see."

While they continued to look on, Kenneth's dreads appeared over the wall, followed by his entire body. Minutes later he had climbed the wall and was standing next to Keenan listening to Fabio's every word.

"Y'all gonna put him down?" he softly asked.

"Man, hell nah," Keenan quickly responded. "We waiting to see what Fabio says, but you know we never pull the plug on a horse. Horses deserve to live just as long as us, man."

He added, "We done built a physical attachment to these horses just like humans."

Kenneth stood silent, staring at Fabio while he examined Pirate's leg. It had been a rough few days for him since he relapsed earlier that week. His rides to Bunny's continued, but seeing Pirate in that condition sobered him up despite the alcohol he'd already consumed that day.

"Okay, I am going to put anti-inflammatory liquid inside the body, okay?" Fabio said while continuing to hold Pirate's leg in his palm. "It will take some of the pain away and then we're going to put cold water for twenty minutes to help pain."

"Let's do it," Keenan said, looking back at the group of guys and giving them a thumbs-up.

Fabio pulled out a cotton swab and rubbed alcohol in it on the side of Pirate's shoulder. "Easy boy," Keenan said as Pirate jumped a little. The IV needle went deep into the horse's skin and pumped anti-inflammatory fluids for the next twenty minutes, followed by a shot of pain medicine.

"Make sure to put some bute on its leg two times tomorrow morning, okay?" Fabio explained to Keenan. "That pain cream will help a lot, and you have to put it once in the morning and once in the afternoon."

"Will do, Fabio," Keenan said.

Fabio believed that Pirate had injured his leg getting in and out of his stall. The wooden barrier that divided the arena from the stall had been slick from the rain and Pirate had slipped. It was an accident, but it also reflected the state of the ranch. Each rain brought new problems. Sometimes the water tore holes in the tin roofs, while other times it deteriorated the structure of the stalls.

At the current rate, the ranch would continue to crumble away with each rainfall, threatening the health and safety of the horses. Donations had run out almost six months ago and the ranch was surviving on its last funds. Randy's attempts to raise money were falling short. Time was running out, and so was everyone's patience.

PBR

RANDY WOKE UP WITH EVERYTHING to be happy about on the morning of the PBR event. A few prominent black bull riders were outside in the arena visiting with members of the cowboys and speaking about their shared interests and love for the sport.

He and the rest of the cowboys had just been invited to the Professional Bull Riders finals at the Staples Center in downtown Los Angeles the day before. They were treated like superstars as they walked around the arena to standing ovations. The Compton Cowboys were becoming the ambassadors for black cowboys in ways that they had only dreamed about.

But something was off with Randy. While the group of black bull riders from Texas continued to speak with Tre outside in the arena, Randy was alone in his room having an emotional breakdown. Tears flowed from his eyes down his face and onto his shoulders as he sat on the brown carpet floor wearing nothing but underwear, holding his head in his hands. The inside of his room was quiet, only catching some of the sounds of loud rap music that blasted in a car outside on the driveway, in competition with thousands of competing thoughts that filled his head.

There was just so much going on. So much going on, and he felt the weight and pressure of the ranch's troubles mounting, and with every small victory, the relief that followed was only temporary. It was enough to make someone go crazy. He kept going back to his family, thinking about how they were all on the line, and how he didn't want to disappoint them. He was figuring things out day to day—the business, the public relations, the guys, and the fate of the ranch.

The tears continued for the next thirty minutes. On the eve of their second day at the PBR event, the support that he and the cowboys had received was hard to process. People stopped them to ask for photos. They knew their names. They knew their horses' names. It was almost like a weird form of guilt, like they didn't deserve it. It was a form of survivor's guilt, the feeling of questioning a sought-after success but then not knowing how to handle it when it comes. The endorsement deals and commercial opportunities were beginning to happen for the cowboys as well. Popular riding brands like Ariat had taken an interest in supporting the Cowboys, helping them become ambassadors for black cowboy culture. Brands like Boot Barn and McDonald's had hired some of the cowboys for commercials. Randy felt conflicted about all of this, because being from Compton, they were so used to being antagonized that it suddenly felt surreal for people to embrace them like this. He had to keep it together. But he didn't know what to tell people who wanted to help—like Mayisha, he too was now struggling to find ways of letting go of control and letting other people in.

When the tears subsided, he wiped his face with a towel. His black cowboy hat and freshly pressed black Compton Cowboys T-shirt sat on his bed next to the signature gold watch, necklace, and bracelet that he would wear that day. He put these on and came back to life, surveying himself in the mirror.

"I ain't playing with these mothafuckers," he said, smiling. "I ain't playin'."

Outside, Tre and Ezekiel Mitchell, a twenty-one-year-old

professional bull rider from a small town in Texas, stood in the center of the arena while Keenan trained Sonny and Fury. The two competitors, though they grew up separated by thousands of miles, had more in common than they had differences. Both had grown up playing football and came from low-income homes.

As some of the few black competitors in a mostly white sport, the two instantly created a brotherhood that stemmed from learning how to compete in their sports by studying and watching YouTube videos.

"Do you know Chris Byrd?" Ezekiel asked.

"Chris?" Tre yelled, laughing. "Man, I went to high school with that fool!"

They both laughed and recognized just how small the black cowboy world was. At twenty-one, Ezekiel was considered one of the top ten riders in the world and on pace to becoming number one.

"Y'all ready to go?" Randy said as he stepped out of his house. The cowboys had to head back to the PBR event, this time to attend a workshop about black cowboys and to meet Charles Sampson, a local hero from Watts, one of the greatest black bull riders of all time.

THE EYES ON each of the cowboys widened as hall of famer Charles "Charlie" Sampson spoke about his experience growing up in Watts.

"Now, we all know that Watts and Compton are very unattractive places to a lot of people in the world," he said while speaking to a group of about thirty black cowboys in attendance for the private workshop. "But even though I was from Watts, and was often the only black competitor, I felt like I had to fit in, all I cared about was becoming the best bull rider I could be. Just like the ones from Texas and Oklahoma," he added.

Eugene, the youngest member of the cowboys, hung on every word that Charles said. "That sounds like me," he said when he learned that Charles's introduction to rodeo was riding ponies in and around Compton. He sat on the edge of his seat as Charles continued to speak about his heralded success in the professional bull riding circuit. Being the first African-American to win the Professional Rodeo Cowboys Association world championship in 1982 was no small feat. Neither was his induction into the hall of fame in 1996.

For Eugene, who came from a riding family of his own, meeting Charles Sampson was a dream. He continued to look around at the transformation of the Staples Center from a basketball arena into a riding arena and wondered about his own future. His family rode horses in Mississippi and were always present in his childhood; to compete in the PRCA as a calf roper had become his personal goal.

What the cowboys saw in Eugene was a younger version of themselves. Eugene was currently at an age when horse riding had helped them cope with the dangers of the streets. They saw someone whom they could mentor and teach.

For Eugene, it was also an age where the importance of the ranch became crystal clear. He too had found a new home there, a place that liberated him from all outside forces and influences. There were no worries on the ranch, just complete freedom.

Moments later, Randy raised his hand to ask Charles a question.

"What are you most excited about with the state of black cowboy culture?" he asked.

"What am I most excited about?" Charles responded with his own question. He took a moment before replying, mulling over the question.

"It's you guys," he finally said.

THE KIDS

KEENAN DIPPED HIS TATTOOED HANDS into the wooden-framed garden bed outside his mother's home. It was still early in the season, but the harvest was on the horizon. Each weed that he dug out from the garden was placed in a growing pile by his feet. His fingers slowly ran through the soil looking for smaller weeds. This time next year, his family would be eating the vegetables from this garden.

It had been months since he had moved back in with his mother. The rising costs of living in Inglewood coupled with unemployment had forced the young family to move out of their apartment there and back to Compton. His wife and daughter were only blocks away, in his mother-in-law's home. Living back on the farms would be a departure from the life he and his wife had imagined for themselves, but being on the ranch was also a way to save money, especially as the couple's first child was only six months away from being born.

Being back on the ranch would also bring him closer to realizing his dream of opening up a small farm in Lancaster with his friend Mike who owned a few acres. They wanted to grow their own vegetables, with the hope of bringing fresh produce to Compton on a weekly basis. After all, the Mexicans were growing their own vegetables and milking their own cows. Why couldn't they do that too? The way Keenan imagined it, they could involve the kids when more of them started coming back to the ranch.

As a chef, he understood the importance of food and healthy

eating. He was brought up in a food desert with limited access to healthy food and vegetables. He wanted to change that. Giving his community access to healthier lifestyles could impact their physical health, too. He couldn't believe that most people had no idea where their food came from, or that they'd never experienced the satisfaction of growing their own. On top of the vegetables that he would be able to grow, living back on the ranch would help him fully commit to ensuring its survival.

As he continued to tend to his garden, he heard the sounds of a few children in the arena who were there for Saturday classes. Their voices reminded him of the past, a time when the ranch was full with as many as fifty kids at any given time.

He listened to the children, thinking about the future of the ranch.

Pirate leaned down and nibbled on a stack of hay in the middle of the arena, surrounded by four piles of fresh dirt that needed to be dumped in the stalls on Monday.

Twelve-year-old Ethan sat next to his brother Isaiah and waited for his turn to answer the questions that were written in front of him on his worksheet. They were accompanied by Star and Lauren, two middle schoolers who lived minutes away from the ranch.

"If something gets stuck in its intestine, they can die from overeating," Ethan said to the group, reading attentively from his worksheet. The two brothers had been part of the Compton Junior Posse in years past, but this was one of their first times back on the ranch. They were with Jamie, a CJP alumnus, who had since taken over the Saturday morning sessions.

Star read from the worksheet and learned about horses in ways that her local Compton school district couldn't teach her.

"If something gets stuck in the intestine," she read while the sound of a police helicopter above the ranch suddenly drained her voice out, "the horse will get . . ."

She stopped reading and looked up at the sky while the helicopter made its way over the ranch, moving in the direction of the courthouse. At this point in their lives, everyone in the circle understood that when the helicopters got too loud, it was time to take a break from reading.

Nearby, in Fury's stable, Randy groomed his horse. His son played in the front house with his mother while she did someone's hair. He looked at the children while he worked and smiled. The youth program was slowly returning to the ranch, and although it didn't have the number of children it once had, it was something nonetheless. What Randy worried about, however, was attracting more at-risk youth in the community—the type of children who would benefit the most from the program. That was critical, not just for the ranch but for the community. Those were the kids who needed the most healing.

At this point, maintaining a positive attitude was all Randy could do since the large donations he had hoped to secure had not come through. Smaller donations, ranging from hundreds of dollars to several thousand, were not enough to sustain the ranch, which as of recently had cost almost twenty-five thousand dollars a month to maintain.

Each child stared at Randy as the helicopter's sound subsided and he finished grooming his horse, preparing her for a ride around the neighborhood. Star, the eleven-year-old daughter of a Mexican mother and an African-American father, smiled and stared the hardest when he walked Fury out into the street.

Next to her, an intense debate was occurring.

"They can definitely die from overeating," Jamie said to Ethan and Isaiah, who had since begun discussing whether or not a horse's ability to poop impacted its chances of survival.

"They can't poop when they—" Jamie said before being cut off by an overzealous Ethan, whose large bifocals were tucked deep into his worksheet.

"Dude, it starts with a C," he told Isaiah, still searching for the answer in his worksheet, the name of one of the intestinal parts of the horse that aided with digestion.

"You mean the cecum?" Jamie finally responded after playfully laughing at the two brothers' brief exchange. "You guys are funny," she added.

Jamie took the group into the arena and grabbed a couple of grooming kits from the shed. "You guys know the safety rules, right?" she said. "Go grab your helmets, and put your horse-riding shoes on too."

"Are we going to ride with saddles or bareback?" Ethan asked.

"Bareback," she said with a smile.

Although Jamie had mostly learned to ride English style, there was no escaping the influence of the Compton style of bareback riding. It was a tradition.

Lauren was reluctant as she stood by Ethan while he brushed Chocolate's body. Her purple sweater, blue jeans, and black Vans stood in deep contrast to the riding shoes and clothes that Ethan was wearing while he groomed the horse. She watched attentively while he cared for the horse, moving closer to him to listen to what he was saying to Chocolate.

"You're a good horse," he whispered into Chocolate's ear, almost the same way Keenan spoke to Sonny. "I'm here to take care of you."

He handed Lauren the brush. "Here, you try."

While they groomed, Xavier, another CJP alumnus, showed up on the ranch. Since he had started working his full-time job, weekends were the only time when he could make it back to help out. Like Jamie, he continued to be pulled back to the ranch.

Xavier and Jamie walked the four young riders around the arena like Mayisha had taught them years before. Theirs was a routine that if performed correctly would eventually replicate itself. It was a routine that would be passed down from rider to rider, from generation to generation.

"Without them there is no program," Jamie said, looking at Ethan coaching Lauren. "They are all that we have."

If finding a purpose for being there wasn't enough, Kenneth's next-door neighbor Sylvester was playing "Reasons" by Earth, Wind & Fire loudly on his speaker system.

The song played loudly while they rode around the arena, barely avoiding the lumps of dirt that stood in the way. Jamie and Xavier had their reasons for taking their time to be at the ranch, and their reasons for wanting to ensure that it survived.

"WE HAVE TO pick up the green stuff too?" Ethan asked.

"Yes, you do," Jamie said while directing Lauren to grab the wheelbarrow and move it toward Chocolate's stall.

Since Anthony had broken his foot earlier in the week in a dirt biking accident, Keenan and Tre had to work on the ranch more often. Keenan had since begun working again, as one of the managers at a local taco restaurant, while Tre continued to balance barber school with rodeo training.

"I'm just going to post up right here and watch y'all," Lauren said while the other three friends stepped inside Chocolate's stall to clean. "I got chased by the Pony last week and it messed me up."

"You know if I ride the Pony my feet will literally touch the ground," Isaiah said while scooping Chocolate's droppings with a shovel into the wheelbarrow.

"Penny is about to get mad at you," Star said to Lauren as she attempted to pet him.

"He looks so nice," Lauren said to Penny while petting his nose. "How about you come help us clean these stalls?"

Everyone in the group laughed, making Tre take a break from cleaning Luke's stall to see what the commotion was about. He smiled when he realized what the kids were laughing about, remembering his first days on the ranch.

"OMG, he's pooping!" Star shouted.

"Last time I was here, I saw that horse pee, and then you walked in it!" Lauren yelled to Isaiah.

"No, I didn't!" he fired back while Penny neighed loudly.

"Is he going to jump over the rail?" Lauren asked.

"No, silly, it's too high for him to jump over," Star replied. "If you try and pet him and lose a finger, don't blame it on me!"

"What's up, bro? Can I pet you?" Lauren asked Penny while standing on the other side of the metal gate.

Penny neighed furiously, making Lauren jump back.

"Oh no!" Star said as she followed Isaiah and Lauren out of the stalls.

Ethan stayed back in Chocolate's stall, eagerly completing the task until he realized his friends had left.

"Hey, wait for me!"

Keenan watched the riders smile and laugh and live out a childhood that he wished he had experienced. These were different types of kids, he thought to himself. These were young people who were never forced to compromise their childhood. They were growing up in a different era when the threat of gang violence wasn't as strong as it was in the past. They liked to ride horses but didn't face the same dangers as Keenan and the rest of the cowboys.

While the youth program slowly began to move forward with the help of many of the cowboys and Junior Posse alumni, the ranch nevertheless continued to slowly deteriorate around them. The Compton Junior Posse sign that for so many years had pleasantly invited visitors into the ranch was slowly falling down. The bottom half had already fallen on the ground next to a pile of loose gravel. Like the community around it, the rest of the sign continued to stand with resilience despite the challenges it faced.

On top of that, seeing the type of kids that the youth program was attracting made Keenan think about who they had to target the program to.

"Our generation of riders were the backyard boogie kids," he said to Anthony while leaning on the metal ranch gate. "We didn't have it this good, which is why it's so funny to see this now. Me and my friends never did schoolwork when we came to the ranch, and we weren't as nice as these kids. We used to be back here cussing and fighting and messing with girls. And we need those types of kids here, too."

After walking around the arena a few times, Lauren looked at the obstacle course with deep confusion. "So, basically we're training like those horses?" she asked Jamie, who while they were riding had set up a course for the group to run around, using the same types of obstacles as for horses.

Everyone laughed at Lauren's question, and the kids began running around the obstacles the same way Chocolate or Sonny would have done.

"I ain't got time for all this!" Lauren said as she trailed behind. "I hope this helps your butt!"

Tre struggled to pull a trash can full of horse droppings across the arena, taking a break in the middle to catch his breath.

"God damn, this shit is heavy," he said, wiping the sweat off his forehead.

Keenan and Tre joined the group and began helping with the saddling and grooming. Keenan helped Lauren clean out Sonny's horseshoes with a hoof pick while Tre helped Star put a saddle on Helio.

"This horse moves a lot," Star said nervously to Tre. He stood a few feet behind him while he tightened up the rope on the metal gate.

"You just have to be calm yourself, if you want the horse to be calm," Tre said, his tone implying that he had handled hundreds of unruly horses in his time. "It's going to be okay, don't be scared."

When the two horses joined together in the middle of the arena, Tre and Keenan began speaking in Jamaican accents that threw the children off.

"You don't see no rasta?" Tre kidded the group in a voice he had been perfecting for years.

"Why you talking like that?" Lauren asked.

"Because me a raaaaasta boy, Kingston, Jamaica," Tre said. "Why you no think meh a rasta boy?"

"Man, you're crazy!" Lauren yelled.

"Meh crazy. Meh crazy about these horses!" he replied, inciting laughs among everyone in the group.

Byron arrived just in time to hear what he thought sounded like people speaking with Jamaican accents in the arena. He wore a short-sleeved green T-shirt and blue jeans that nearly covered

his burgundy red Chuck Taylor shoes. He smoked a Black &
Mild cigar.

"What t-t-the hell is g-g-going on over there?" he said out
loud, while Destiny, a six-year-old girl who had been sitting under the shaded canopy, watched on.

"Oh, hello," Byron said to Destiny.

"Hi," she replied.

Tre's championship belt shone in the sun as he barked directions. "So, the half circle is basically to space y'all out," he said,
walking backward as the youth riders began to ride in a circle
by themselves. "We have to maintain good spacing and keep all
of the horses the same distance from one another. Everyone try
to stay as close to the rails as possible. The bigger the circle you
make the longer the circle has to be."

The riders slowly pulled the reins on their horses and moved
closer to the rails while they rode.

"Just keep kissing and kicking," Tre said, explaining the sounds
that they needed to make with their mouths to make the horses
move forward at a steady pace.

ALRIGHT, THEN

THOUGH MIMI LOVED HORSES, SHE almost never joined Keiara at the ranch, preferring to stay in the comfort of her home. But the day wasn't an ordinary one. It was the last time her granddaughter and great-granddaughter would be at the ranch for the foreseeable future.

Keiara had decided it was time to move back to Houston. She was at the ranch to say goodbye to her horse, her friends, and the cowboys. It had always been her dream to return to Texas, but life, and the eventual birth of Taylor, had altered her plans.

"Houston is where I've always been able to grow and blossom," she said while leaning on her grandmother's shoulder. Al Green's "Love and Happiness" played on her cell phone on the table in front of her. "I always see myself ending up there." Whenever she was there her mind felt free, so immersed in the city's black cowboy culture. It was like no other place in the world. A place where nobody looked twice if they saw a black woman wearing a cowboy hat.

Nearby, a few of her close friends and their children had gathered and sat reminiscing about their time together. Like the black-inked tattoo of a cross that covered Keiara's arm and extended down into her hand, her move to Texas was also inspired by faith in something that she could not yet see but believed deep in her soul.

Keiara wasn't as prepared to move to Houston as she would have liked to be. She didn't have a job lined up and would have to rely on her close friend Jazmine, a black woman who also competed in rodeo, to accommodate her and Taylor until she could find housing and earn money from competing on the circuit.

This time she had Penny and Taylor and was even more committed to becoming the first black woman at the national finals than ever.

"This move is bringing me one step closer to my dream," she said to her grandmother, as more of her friends and family began to arrive at the ranch. "God brought me back to Compton when my brother was killed, and I didn't fight it, but now he's taking me back to Texas." She'd been waiting for this for the past five years.

While Keiara's excitement was palpable, she knew her grandmother might suffer from her pursuit of her dream. With her gone, it would be difficult to find someone to drive Mimi to and from her medical appointments. But Mimi wanted Keiara to pursue her dream. She urged her to leave.

Randy joined the group, carrying a large box of fried chicken and potato wedges for everyone to share. Keiara's absence would be felt throughout the ranch. Though their strong personalities often clashed, seeing her leave was like watching one of his relatives go. To show love and support, Randy had offered to trailer her horse Penny to Houston the following week.

While the group of friends continued to hang out by the arena, Eugene and Tre practiced their roping on a wooden bull nearby, while a trio of farriers worked on some of the horses' shoes. At this time of year, the white farrier had been replaced by two high-school-aged Latinos and a black man. While they worked, Byron appeared on the ranch and looked intently while one of the men grabbed the horse's hoof and trimmed it before shoeing it. His eyes widened like it was his first time seeing a horseshoe replacement in his life.

Taylor frolicked with her cousin Melrose in the arena. The two friends happily played around one of the dirt mounds, unaware that this would be one of their last times on the ranch together. They ran around the arena, imitating the horses nearby.

"Horsiieeeeee," Taylor yelled as Penny trotted away from her.

Taylor would be too young to remember what the ranch meant to her and the peace her mother felt when she brought her there. But even in Houston, Keiara wanted her daughter never to forget about the city that they had both survived.

Keiara looked at Taylor while she galloped around the arena. Her daughter's milk chocolate skin and pigtails reminded her of herself when she was her age. While Compton's own black riding legacy ran in her blood, moving Taylor to a city where black cowboys and cowgirls were the norm was, in her mind, worth the struggle. Together, they were a team, and they'd grown used to adapting to new situations. Keiara felt this was almost like a form of training—that she'd put Taylor through a lot, but the reward was that they'd reach a permanent place of stability in Texas.

At the end of the day, she thought, if your dream doesn't scare you, then it isn't a big enough dream.

Moments later, one of her friends pulled out a bottle of Patrón tequila, Keiara's drink of choice, and suddenly the mood of the group went from quiet and pensive to cheerful. "Oh, I hope y'all didn't think you weren't going to take any shots with me on my last day?" Keiara said with a full smile. "You know I'm not going to see y'all for a while, so, girls, let's get these shots in!"

AFTER THEY SAID their goodbyes to Keiara, Tre drove in the direction of the riding arena in Palos Verdes while Eugene sat in the passenger seat, looking out at the world around him as they crossed Compton's borders. Dilapidated residential homes with potholed streets and graffiti-covered walls were replaced by verdant eucalyptus trees, lush gardens, and well-maintained roads as they approached the opulent Palos Verdes community.

A typical membership at the Palos Verdes arena could cost upward of five thousand dollars for initiation and an eight-hundred-dollar monthly fee. But with the help of Big Al and Terry, two older black riders who knew Tre's father, Tre and Eugene and other local Compton riders got the chance to use the state-of-the-art facilities for calf-roping practice throughout the week.

The practice session was divided into two sections. The first half involved riding a horse and simulating roping the calf, while the second involved running toward a roped calf, flipping it on its back, and quickly tying its legs up with a rope. Though Tre preferred bareback riding over calf roping, it was becoming one of his favorite events the more time he spent with Al and Terry.

"You ready to go?" Al asked Tre, who stood by the metal door waiting for the calf to shoot out of it on Al's remote-controlled command.

"Yep, let's do it," Tre responded.

Al pressed the button and within seconds the calf was released into the arena. It ran full speed ahead while Tre sprinted toward it with reckless abandon and chased it down the same way he had successfully done in arenas around the country for the past few years. When he reached the calf, he slammed his knee into the calf's chest and flipped its body into the air, using the force of both of his arms before tossing it on its side and tying its legs with a rope.

"Whew!" Tre yelled into the air, still panting from the rush of adrenaline that flowed through his body while the calf lay roped in front of him.

Al proudly looked at Tre while he got up from the ground and walked back in his direction. "Not bad," he said. "You're pretty fast, but I bet I can beat you in the forty-yard dash."

Tre looked at Al with a smile. "Man, you're crazy."

"Okay, maybe not the forty, but how about a ten-yard dash?" Al responded.

Terry and Eugene and the rest of the guys laughed at Al's wishful thinking.

"Tre, you look a bit tired," Terry said to Tre. He clenched an unsmoked cigar in his hand, still leaning on the gate as the sun continued to set. "Boy, at your age you aren't supposed to be tired!"

The group of friends continued to practice until the sun set on the eucalyptus trees that surrounded the arena. It felt like paradise, because it was—it was cowboy paradise, for a group of cowboys from Compton.

KEIARA WALKED AROUND her apartment the next morning still wearing her black head wrap from the previous night. She wasn't in her early twenties anymore. She couldn't hang like she used to. In a day she and Taylor would be boarding a plane to Houston, far away from the only community her daughter had ever called home.

Keiara's biggest headache had been finding a way to move her horse to Houston, but when Randy and Tre offered to drive Penny for her, things suddenly became much easier for the twenty-nine-year-old single mother. They were saving her the nine hundred dollars it would have cost her to rent a trailer.

Moving in with her childhood friend Jazmine Bennett was another deciding factor for her move. The two friends had both dreamed about making the national finals since they were children, and with each other to rely on for support, their dreams finally seemed attainable.

"She's one of the few people that rides horses out there that I know," Keiara said. "But a lot of people out there believe in me, and I know I'm not going to have a stall when I get there. My back is still injured, but I have faith in God that it'll all work out even though a lot of people here are doubting my decision to leave."

She didn't have a job lined up, but she had a dream, and for Keiara, that was more than enough.

"My journey in Compton is done, and to know that some riders in Houston believe in me is a blessing," she said. "I don't feel the same love here and I know all that I've been going through is to help me make and become one of the first black women in the national rodeo finals."

TAYLOR HURRIED BACK down from the upstairs bedroom and into the living room to find her favorite Saturday morning film, *Frozen*, still on the big-screen television. It had now been a few days since she and Keiara had arrived in Cypress, a suburb filled with housing developments, forty minutes northwest of Houston. Both were slowly adjusting to the pace of their new lives.

Taylor had grown accustomed to sleeping with the sounds of the police helicopters and sirens that echoed throughout Compton. The stillness of the Texas nights made her uneasy and she found herself nervously reaching for Keiara's touch her first few nights in Cypress.

As Keiara and Taylor drove to Dairy Queen earlier that morning, the gravity of the move finally dawned on her as their car passed vast fields of green. Unlike the Richland Farms, the pasture seemed to stretch for miles without an end in sight. "Shit, man," Keiara said to herself, "it's for real now."

Watching *Frozen* every morning since she arrived was the closest thing to the schedule Taylor had back in Compton. She yelled at the screen like it was her first time seeing the movie. But living in a home with other people, including Jazmine's two daughters and her brother, meant that it would no longer be just her and her mother. In addition, Jazmine's mother, a Compton-bred woman from Mimi's generation, lived nearby and enforced a strict napping and eating schedule every time she was at the house, filling part of the gap created by Mimi's absence.

With two stories, several bedrooms, a garage, and a backyard that led directly into a two-hundred-acre pasture with grazing cows, Jazmine's house was the largest home that Keiara and Taylor had ever lived in. Having a place that size was something she had wanted for Taylor, and though she knew their stay with Jazmine was temporary, the idea of owning something similar was part of her dream.

With the money that she had saved and the rodeo purses she could earn at weekend barrel racing events, it would be months before she would be able to afford to move out, and although Jazmine urged her to find a part-time job in the meantime, rodeo was the only thing that she had come to Texas to do. Jazmine took it upon herself to do everything in her power to help Keiara and Taylor adjust. Though they weren't related by blood, the two considered each other sisters after having lived in each other's homes at different points in their lives.

Jazmine had made the journey from Compton to Houston almost ten years before. She had arrived on a bus with two duffel bags full of clothes, a saddle, and a hundred dollars in her pocket.

It was the look in Keiara's eyes that she understood—a blend of desire and sacrifice, part of the code that she had learned riding horses on the farms. Jazmine also worried that at some point reality would kick her sister harder than a Thoroughbred. Rodeo was a gamble, and to succeed, you had to spend money to make money. Sometimes competitors wouldn't bring back home any purses. Sometimes they would leave with hundreds of dollars in fees down the drain. At some point, Keiara would have to learn about this on her own, but until then all Jazmine could do was support her sister's dream.

As one of the best and most respected female rodeo competitors in the state, Jazmine also understood what it felt like to come from a city where rodeo wasn't as widely accepted as it was in Texas. She also got tired of having to explain that people in California didn't just surf, they competed in rodeo as well.

In California, the women's rodeo circuit was not as fully integrated into the Women's Professional Rodeo Association as it was in Texas. The WPRA was a diverse organization to which most black women rodeo competitors in Houston belonged, and it helped create the camaraderie the competitors shared. People wanted to see each other win in ways that didn't happen in California. Maybe it was that rodeo had a stronger cultural lineage in Texas, or maybe it was that in California, rodeo competitors had fewer chances to compete and were fighting for scraps. In Texas, black rodeos were made for entire families to attend. They were as much about holding on to a piece of history as they were about ensuring the future of black rodeo life.

Two of Jazmine's light brown saddles proudly sat on a chair next to the television with the inscription "2016 Ladies Barrel Racing Champion" on both sides. Taylor wasn't at the age where she could understand what the inscription on the saddles meant, or understand the amount of blood, sweat, and tears that went into winning the championship that year. She was too young to know that Jasmine and her mother were part of the last generation of riders from Compton—too young to understand that her mother's desire to be a champion was the very reason why she had decided to move her from their home.

Still, something about Jazmine's saddles drew Taylor in. She played with them, presciently outlined each letter with her tiny index finger, perhaps dreaming of her own life as a future rodeo champion.

Keiara rubbed her hand across the tattoo of Mimi's name on her right arm as Taylor played with the saddles. She thought about what her grandmother was doing that morning. Living thousands of miles away from Mimi didn't stop Keiara from communicating with her a few times a day. Living in Cypress sometimes felt like a transplanted version of Compton, especially when Keiara cooked the meatloaf and greens that Mimi had taught her how to make while reruns of *Martin* played loudly on the television as familiar Compton slang that only they knew rolled smoothly from their tongues.

BACK IN COMPTON, the cowboys were also leaning heavily on hope. The future of the ranch was uncertain, and because the ranch restoration project that Randy had designed never gained the traction he had hoped for, he realized that keeping it alive would require the same community effort that had once made it succeed more than thirty years ago.

Every meeting with a potential sponsor and donor could have been the answer to the ranch's financial woes. Not securing funding, however, didn't deter them from continuing to be the change that they wanted to see in the community. Even if every horse had to get sold, the cowboys weren't going to go down without a fight.

But the hardship that the ranch was experiencing was, ironically, doing more to bring the cowboys together than it did to keep them apart. When Myron, one of the original black riders from the farms, heard that the ranch was starting to crumble, he, alongside other members of the community, joined the cowboys in helping to build new stables and install new panels.

Myron looked at the skin of the shirtless tattooed men who worked together to lift the heavy metal panels from one side of the ranch to the other. Sweat poured from their bodies as they worked to improve their ranch the way cowboys on the farms and throughout the South had done for centuries. These were the same shirtless boys who had stared in awe at Myron and the other black riders when they would dress up in tailored western-style clothing on Sundays.

"LORD, PLEASE BLESS this rodeo and help us ensure that everyone who competes today walks away as healthy as they arrived and leaves without injury. Lord, we ask you bless on this holy day and continue to bless us," the announcer said into a microphone from a room high above the arena. "Okay, it's time to rodeo!"

Though it would be months before Keiara's back injury would allow her to compete, the announcer's words brought her the biggest smile of the day. If she were back in Compton, she would have been at home on a Sunday. But in Texas, every weekend brought a new rodeo, sometimes several in one day.

Jazmine's youngest daughter, Kaidence, and Taylor watched closely while Jazmine and other women prepared their horses and rode around the arena, their friends and family watching from the bleachers. The riders loosened the reins on each of their horses and made kissing sounds from their pursed lips while their hooves made fresh tracks throughout the arena. Keiara watched and wished she was healthy enough to ride but knew that everything worked in God's time. Part of her wished that her brother was still alive to see her move closer to her dream. But another part of her knew that Jerrod—and other black men like Black, Marcus, and Slim, and the ghosts of other fallen Compton cowboys—would be with her wherever she went.

The sound of zydeco music continued to play loudly on overused speakers, moving the hips of black cowboys and cowgirls as it had for decades. An elderly couple danced together near their pickup truck while holding on tightly to the brims of their beige Stetson hats, drawing cheers from onlookers. The smell of some of the county's best barbecue came out of someone's smoking grill and wafted into the sky. A familiar laugh from an unfamiliar face caused her to look in its direction. Everything in Keiara's life was perfect. The sounds, the smells—it all felt like home because, in more ways than she could ever know, it all was home.

AUTHOR'S NOTE

THE 11TH COWBOY

THE STORY OF COMPTON'S BLACK cowboys never left my mind. It had been years since I had seen them as a child, but as a *New York Times* reporter, I decided to investigate. To my astonishment, the cowboys I remembered were still there. Though the cowboys I had seen growing up near Compton were no longer riding their horses through the city, there was a new generation of young black men who were. This time, however, they called themselves the "Compton Cowboys." I stumbled upon their Instagram account and slid into their DMs, hoping they would respond to my request for an interview, which they did. It wasn't long before I realized the mission that they had embarked on: this group of black men weren't only riding horses as a hobby—they were riding them as a way to stay alive and to eradicate stereotypes about black cowboys and their city, proudly proclaiming their motto, "Streets raised us. Horses saved us."

Before going on leave from the *New York Times* to write this book in 2018, I was working on stories in countries throughout the world. I was part of a team called "Surfacing" at the *Times* that specifically worked on stories about global subcultures. My schedule was erratic, and I was traveling the world writing stories about communities who lived at the margins of different societies. It all seemed surreal, particularly for a kid from Southeast

L.A. who had spent countless hours watching and dreaming about the airplanes that flew above my home as they landed at the nearby Los Angeles International Airport. After working on the Compton Cowboys' story in February, I moved on to a story about an albino community in Ghana who were fighting to stay alive while being hunted for their body parts by witch doctors and rural villagers. In April of that year, I traveled to Japan with a *New York Times* film crew to host a show about the experiences of the Japanese lowrider community in Tokyo and Nagoya. I had also worked on a story about a group of inspiring women rappers from the city of Oaxaca, Mexico, who were using rap music as a way to speak out against the killing of women throughout that state. In total, I had traveled to about eight different countries and worked on ten stories in the span of eight months. Every story that I worked on that year simultaneously brought me closer to understanding how infinitely complex the human experience was and took me farther away from the ranch in Richland Farms, which I continued to visit whenever I was back in L.A.

Coming back home to write this book meant that I would be temporarily leaving my position at the *Times*. But returning to Southeast Los Angeles for an extended amount of time also meant that I would be coming back a different person. My travels around the world as a subculture reporter had deeply impacted the perceptions I had about myself and the communities that I came from. Each story brought me closer to understanding that in my struggle to belong at different points in my life, I was never truly alone. I realized there were countless other people who navigated the same questions that I did. At times, I felt many of the same feelings that Kendrick Lamar, my favorite rapper, sang about in his award-winning album *To Pimp a Butterfly*. Like him, I also felt a deep sense of survivor's guilt, that I'd been one of the lucky ones to "make it out of the 'hood," and even fortunate enough to have traveled so much of the world in a way that I never imagined I would ever do. I struggled to understand why *I* was given the opportunity to travel to so many different countries, meet so many different types of people, and gain a perspective of my place in the vastness of the world. Coming back to L.A. also helped me realize what Kendrick felt when he spoke about coming back home to a reality filled with violence and hardship. I often felt isolated from my friends and family and felt completely disconnected from the community that had taught me so many things as a youth. The isolation that I felt would crystallize into sporadic bouts of depression that I would conceal from my friends and family. I felt confused about the issues that continued to impact my community, and what working for a company like the *New York Times* meant for my life.

One of the hardest things to reconcile was that working for the *Times* didn't stop me from being racially profiled in the streets by the police. In the context of the streets, working for the *Times* didn't mean anything. Being back home and working on this book in Compton every day served as a harsh reminder that the status symbols that I had picked up along the way—Stanford education, awards, media recognition, a *New York Times* email address—didn't stop bullets from coming in my direction from the guns of people who looked like me. One day in early October, I joined Anthony, Terrance, and Keenan on a ride around the farms. It was about 1:30 in the afternoon and it had been months since the three friends had ridden together. Minutes into the ride, as I struggled to keep up with the fast pace of their horses, we were stopped by a police officer driving in an unmarked Los Angeles Sheriff's Department car.

The police officer turned his lights on and told us to "pull over," using the loudspeaker inside his car. Me and the guys looked at one another and immediately chuckled. How the hell did he want us to pull over? I was on foot holding a large DSLR camera in one hand and a voice recorder in the other, and the guys were on their horses, riding on the right side of the street.

"He wants us to do what?" Anthony asked with a bewildered look on his face. "We're already on the side of the road!" he yelled to the oncoming police car. When the officer finally pulled up to us moments later, an African-American middle-aged officer with a salt-and-pepper goatee rolled down his window and looked at us in astonishment.

"What the hell are you guys doing on those horses?" he asked in an aggressive but playful tone. "You know damn well black people aren't supposed to be on no damn horses!" he said, chuckling to himself. Nobody—including myself—laughed at his joke. Keenan and Terrance cautiously looked at the officer from behind Anthony's horse. After what seemed like an eternity, Anthony looked around. "We're different," he finally said, with an immense amount of pride as the police officer finally drove away. "We're different."

"We're different" is a sentiment that I continued to feel from the cowboys as I spent more time on the ranch and became embedded in their lives. Many of them had been ridiculed by their friends and family for riding horses, yet they continued to ride anyway. Every cowboy rode for different reasons. But each rode horses because it healed them *and* healed members of their families and their community. Being soft could easily get you killed in Compton, but softness was also one of the most valuable currencies inside the ranch.

Still, there was something else that connected me to their lives. I felt drawn to their story because, in many ways, I, too, was challenging a perceived stereotype. My first week at the *New York Times* office in Manhattan revealed a particular truth: I looked very different from the other reporters who sat with me during our two-day orientation. Most of them weren't young, weren't black or brown, didn't wear brightly colored Nike Air Max shoes, and didn't get their haircuts in a Compton barbershop like I did. The first time I drove to the ranch, I was met with some apprehension because of my appearance. Except for Randy, whom I had chatted with on Instagram, nobody knew what I looked like prior to meeting me. When I pulled up to Caldwell Street in my grey 2009 Toyota Prius playing Kendrick Lamar's *Good Kid, M.A.A.D City* album loud enough to be heard outside my car, none of the guys expected someone who looked like me to work for the *New York Times*.

"Who you looking for?" Carlton asked me as I stood on the other side of the double-bolted metal door in my 1995 Air Maxes, blue denim jeans, and black crewneck sweater.

"I spoke to Randy on the phone and he said to be here at 3:30 for the interview," I quickly responded, speaking to the metal door, still unaware of who I was talking to. "My name is Walter and I'm a reporter with the *New York Times*." Carlton finally opened the door but was still on the fence about who I was, so he proceeded with caution and took another glance at me—this time a much closer one. After a minute had passed, I suddenly remembered that I had prepared for this moment earlier in the day. Before heading to the ranch that afternoon, I had stacked my wallet—as I always did—with about ten company-issued business cards that had my name, contact information, and, most importantly, occupation: *New York Times* reporter. This wasn't the first time something like this had happened; people always gave me the craziest looks whenever I mentioned what I did for a living. When Carlton continued to size me up, I reached into my wallet and handed him a business card.

"Ohhhh . . . THE *New York Times*," he said with a cheerful smile as he read the name on the card. "Walter Thompson-Hernández," he read out slowly, enunciating every word. "Yeah, Randy had said a reporter was coming to the ranch today, but, shit, my nigga, I didn't think he would look like you!" After we exchanged a laugh and gave each other a firm handshake-hug combo, he welcomed me inside his home, where we waited for the rest of the guys to arrive.

The Compton Cowboys were expecting a middle-aged white man that day. They were expecting someone who, according to Keenan, had "a more serious vibe." Never in their wildest dreams (or mine) did they think that a young man of color who grew up minutes away from them would be representing one of the most prestigious newspapers in the world. That nobody believed me was both disheartening and hilarious. I mean, given the perception of the *Times,* I couldn't really blame them. I walked and talked just like members of the group. I was black too. It almost automatically gave me access into their world in a way that no white, middle-aged reporter could have achieved. These men and I had grown up shopping at the same markets with our mothers, most of us had absent fathers, we listened to the same Tupac records as kids and cried the day we learned he had been killed. We learned not to wear certain colors because those attracted danger.

We had also both felt represented by Kendrick's *Good Kid, M.A.A.D City* album. Every song on that album reflected some aspect of my life and the lives each cowboy had experienced as young black men in the city of Compton. One day on the ranch while speaking with Keenan about the book, I explained to him how much *Good Kid, M.A.A.D City* had meant to me and how often I listened to it while writing this book. He looked at me for a moment and then said, "Well, you're right, that album is us. We're the good kids in a mad city."

Still, as a reporter with graduate school training in ethnography, there was something inherently different about the way I would have to tell this story. Reporting it meant that I would have to fully immerse myself into the cowboys' lives. The little over a year I spent with them at the ranch writing this book, taking photographs and making observational notes, as I was trained to do as an ethnographer, helped me understand the important role I would have in telling this story. I didn't have the privilege of easily removing myself from the cowboys or the ranch; I had formed intimate bonds with each person in the group. Throughout the course of the year that I spent with them, there were so many moments when I completely forgot that I was there to write a book. It felt like I was hanging out with guys I had known my entire life. Part of the challenge, though, was to write about the group in a way that I hadn't been trained to do. I was taught that I was the expert, but time in the field in different parts of the world had taught me otherwise. The cowboys were the experts in their own story, and that challenged traditional reporting. Reporters and ethnographers often didn't have to deliberately stand back from the groups that they were documenting because they already weren't a part of these communities. Most parachuted into a community and left as soon as they got the information or sound bites they needed. I, on the other hand, had a different relationship to this group. I was both a participant and an observer.

The first time Kenneth relapsed on alcohol, I went to visit him at his home. There was a rumor going around on the ranch that he had been drinking again, and I wanted to find out if it was true. It was almost noon when I arrived at his house, and he had just woken up from a deep slumber. His mouth and his body reeked of booze and there were empty bottles throughout his living room. As a writer, I wanted to understand the reasons for his relapse. I felt like it would be an important part of the book, particularly because of the tension his drinking was creating for the group. But as his friend, there was something inside me that began feeling uncomfortable halfway through the interview as my audio recorder and notepad lay on the table in front of me. It was almost sacrilegious to turn off the recorder, for fear of missing out on important anecdotes, but I did so anyway and stopped taking notes ten minutes into our conversation. When he invited me to accompany him to go buy more booze, I felt conflicted and even more uncomfortable. Even though reporters lived for revealing moments like these, I wanted to help him get back on track. I thought about the men on both sides of my family who had suffered from alcoholism and the effects it had on their lives. I thought about my own paternal grandfather, Walter Thompson, a talented reporter and writer for the *Oakland Tribune* and television host, whose genius and creative gifts had been deeply hindered by his dependency on alcohol.

Every time I came back from an assignment abroad, I would immediately drive to the ranch the following day. There was something about the ranch that kept pulling me back in. It almost felt umbilical. The connection I felt to the cowboys and to the ranch blossomed with each visit. When I was abroad, I would send the guys photos from my travels. It felt like they were with me wherever I was. Anthony, in particular, grew especially fond of hearing about the countries where I was covering stories, because, I believed, he felt that he had been denied the chance to travel due to the choices he made during his youth.

One day, after a work trip to Ghana, I was at the ranch and

checked my wallet to see if I had any money to give to Byron, who had just asked me for fifty cents. I had just gotten back the day before and my wallet was still full of Ghanaian cedis, which Anthony immediately noticed. His eyes widened when he realized that the human faces on each of the bills were black. It was his first time seeing currency with black faces on it. I handed him one of the bills and he examined it thoroughly. "This is wild," he said to me while turning the bill around a few times and putting it above his head so that the sun could shine through it. "These is some black people on these bills! Black people!" he yelled into the air, overjoyed. I was almost brought to tears by the sight as I could only imagine what it must have felt like for Anthony to experience something like that. After that day I began bringing him money from every country I traveled to. I brought him money from Taiwan, Japan, the Dominican Republic, Mexico, New Zealand, and other countries. He began collecting the bills, and they became part of a growing international currency collection that he kept in his home.

The Compton Cowboys became an integral part of my life in ways that I could never have imagined. I attended weekly dinners with Kenneth and his family and walked alongside Anthony while he rode his horse to pick up his granddaughter from her school in Watts. When some of the guys needed to go and pick up more marijuana at the local dispensary, I accompanied them. We often went to eat at Cliff's or Mom's, two well-known local fast-food establishments. During Tre's professional rodeo season, I accompanied him to rodeos throughout California. We shared many moments at the ranch together and often found ourselves at the Louisiana Fried Chicken fast-food restaurant on Alondra Boulevard and Wilmington Avenue where Keenan almost lost Sonny. When Keiara and her daughter, Taylor, went to ride at the horse stables in Gardena, I accompanied them and watched as Taylor held on tight to the reins and cried whenever Keiara tried to get her off the horse. Keiara invited me to hang out with her and her friends and her grandmother Mimi at their home in North Long Beach on different occasions. I also went with her to Houston when she first moved there with Taylor to compete in rodeo full-time. Charles confided in me about the legal battle that he and his baby mother were involved in. Randy took many of the moments that we shared alone to voice his fears and concerns for the future in ways that he could not do publicly. He cried in front of me on several occasions as the pressure of keeping the ranch alive began to unfold before his very eyes. As time passed, I invited the cowboys to my birthday parties and to a number of family events. We became close. I went from being a reporter to someone who was considered a part of the group, perhaps the 11th cowboy.

Some of the best moments I experienced were when the recorder that I carried with me at all times was turned off. Or when I left my camera in the car or at home. These moments reminded me of the days I had spent growing up in Los Angeles and many of the childhood friends whom I was no longer in contact with. Being on the ranch also reminded me of my own relationship to horses and farm life, when my mother would send me to our family's rural hometown in Mexico every summer to be with my family. Horses and farm work were a big part of my days during those summer breaks. They are moments I'll remember forever.

When Slim passed away earlier in the summer from a fatal motorcycle accident, I also felt the pain of the cowboys' loss. Though I never got the chance to meet him, I knew what it felt like to lose a close friend. Throughout my life, several close friends had become victims of gun violence. Each affected me, but none as bad as the loss of my best friend, Danny, who was shot and killed at a bus stop near his home in South Central when we were fourteen. Or my other childhood friend Bryan, who was shot and killed over a gold necklace the day he turned twenty-seven, or my close high school friend Oscar, a youth minister, who was shot in the head in front of his home in Venice after being mistaken for a rival gang member.

The Compton Cowboys' story ended up being more than just an improbable tale about a group of black cowboys in one of the most stigmatized communities in the world. It became a story about the power of friendship, love, pain, and the need to have spaces where we go to find healing. What became clear was that as I grew closer to the horses, I, too, was being healed from the trauma that I had experienced during my youth. As the year progressed, I began to take notice of the cultural moment that their story existed in. The Compton Cowboys' mission to eradicate negative stereotypes about African-American cowboys was occurring in one of the most racially and politically divisive moments in modern history. Being a black cowboy in Compton—in the context of the Black Lives Matter movement—increased the stakes of their mission. Black people continued to be killed in America's streets by white police officers with impunity, and though their horses offered a semblance of protection in Compton, riding also came with heightened risks. Horses provided the Compton Cowboys with a form of protection that other people in the 'hood didn't have, but it never fully guaranteed that they would return home safely after each ride.

The cowboys had also directly and indirectly sparked a growing awareness of black cowboys throughout the United States and in music and popular culture. Solange, an award-winning recording artist, was inspired by the Compton Cowboys to create a visual album honoring the experiences of black cowboys in Texas. Similarly, Lil Nas X, a musician and black cowboy, had the smash number one *Billboard* song of the year with "Old Town Road." Houston-native Megan Thee Stallion also emerged on the scene the same year, adorned in cowboy hats, and instantly became a music sensation.

The cowboys, as these events show, were never alone. They continued to fight to preserve cultures that had been part of their families for generations. Social media often helped forge these connections, and as the Compton Cowboys' platform grew, so did their reach. Black cowboys and cowgirls from around the country began to rally to fight and preserve sacred traditions in an increasingly modern world. But the fight didn't end there. The biggest enemy for most of the black urban cowboys whom I spoke to around the United States was how difficult it was to find the resources for their stables and ranches—trying to keep their valuable land out of the hands of wealthy developers.

Gentrification and demographic shifts had caused a deep wound that as Langston Hughes once wrote, "festered like a sore" in the black U.S. cowboy community. In Philadelphia, local riders fought with the city to preserve their ranches amid rapid city-wide development that threatened their way of life. In Baltimore and Oakland, riders also faced the threat of gentrification, often forcing them to abandon horses and move out in search of more affordable housing. In Compton, amid the threat of rising housing costs, the ranch fought to remain the last standing black cowboy ranch in the city. Though it had survived through gang wars, crack cocaine epidemics, and many deaths, still, amid the ongoing struggles, I learned that the ranch was more than a place to care for horses. It ultimately became one of the last places in the farms where black bodies could go to be free—unencumbered by the threat of violence and displacement. It was more than a horse ranch, it was an ecosystem and a safe haven for both the cowboys and me.

ACKNOWLEDGMENTS

I SPENT MOST OF THE year living with my Tia Licha in Huntington Park in the home where I was born and raised. Her daily 5 a.m. alarm, which was always a fast-paced reggaeton song, was the reminder I needed to get up and to start writing. It was also helpful to be so close to my Tia Meche, my other aunt, one of the wisest and biggest santeras on the block. Her blessings *definitely* helped me finish this book. My Tio Eve, my mother's older brother, also lived a few blocks away and reminded me of the power of imagination and good spirit. *Los quiero mucho a los tres.*

I'm grateful for the friends and colleagues and loved ones that read early drafts of this book: Taj, Junot, Tiffany, my mom, my pops, Sara, Fernando, Stephen, Francis. Alex, Lo, Sal, Cesar, and June. I'm grateful for those friends who shared a meal with me or checked in with me through text or phone calls or sent me a DM during the writing process. Writing is isolating and knowing I had a support system was incredibly helpful. I hope I'm as good as a friend as you've all been to me.

My *New York Times* editors, Joanna Nikas and Monica Drake, supported this story from its inception. Joanna, you're a real one. Monica, thank you for your vision and continued support. My Surfacing colleagues, Malin Fezehai and Stephen Hiltner, are two of the most talented storytellers I know, and I'm lucky that our paths crossed that year.

Chad Luibl, my literary agent, thank you for guiding me through this entire process. I hope we can continue to do this for a really long time. Rachel Kahan, my editor at William Morrow, you're one of the best and realest editors in the game. I appreciate you. I'd also like to thank everyone at Morrow, including Kelly Rudolph and Maureen Cole for their publicity strategy, Benjamin Steinberg and Molly Waxman for the marketing campaign, Ploy Siripant for designing the book jacket, and Alivia Lopez for keeping everything running smoothly. Without your help this book would not have been possible.

I've had some incredible professors along the way who have helped shape the manner in which I approach story and narrative. Even though ethnography has a murky past, and a history in colonization and, by extension, the exploitation of communities of color, I've always considered ethnography to be the best approach for the work that I do. I think the only way to try to understand someone's lived experience is to spend quality time with them, to ask questions, and, more importantly, to listen. The trust that I am often given—the access into different worlds—comes with an incredible amount of responsibility. That said, I've learned from some of the very best. University of Southern California (USC) sociologist and professor Pierrette Hondagneu-Sotelo, you've taught me so much about how to write and think about place and belonging. Manuel Pastor, also a sociologist at the University of Southern California (USC) and director at the Program for Environmental and Regional Equity (PERE), thank you for allowing me to learn from you and the other researchers at the center during my two-year stint there. Also, big shout-out to my adopted Tia, Rhonda Ortiz, the managing director at the center. *Gracias por todo.*

Before attending Stanford University, I worked in a mental health hospital as a program counselor for two years near my old home in Venice. I ran programs for a group of twelve Latino residents in a lockdown facility that housed seventy-seven residents who were diagnosed with schizophrenia. I filled out their medication paperwork, acted as a mediator between them and their conservators, coordinated daily workshops, and spent countless hours asking residents questions about their symptoms and lives. Every day was unlike the previous day and no two days were alike during my two years there. I sat in on countless sessions with psychologists and psychiatrists and the more I sat in on these sessions, the more I realized that I was taking a master course in note taking and writing and observation. The lives of the residents that I looked after depended on the notes that I took of them while they sat in sessions and walked throughout the hospital. So much of what I learned during my two years there, I continue to carry with me wherever I go. Sometimes I find myself thinking about some of the hospital's residents while on assignments. And the ways they would respond to some of the very same questions that I continue to ask people today. I'll always be grateful for the realization that although I worked at the hospital and was in service for their needs, it was the residents who left the biggest impact on me. It was one of the most challenging and most beautiful experiences that I've ever had.

I was grateful to study under professors Gary Segura, H. Samy Alim, Tomás Jiménez, and Al Camarillo while I studied at Stanford. I am also forever grateful to Stanford professor Stephen "Sensei" Murphy-Shigematsu, who taught me how to incorporate compassion and mindfulness into research and storytelling. I hope some of the pages in this book reflect some of your sacred teachings. I'm deeply thankful for your guidance and continued friendship.

While writing this book, I also found myself reading. Kiese Laymon's book *Heavy* helped me worked through some of the scenes in this book that at times may have seemed autobiographical. The honesty throughout that book is inspiring and beautiful. Matthew Desmond's book *Evicted* reads like a master class in ethnography. The attention to detail and the worlds that he introduced us to throughout the book felt three-dimensional and nuanced.

This book contains real depictions of death and violence. I've lost several close friends and relatives to gun violence: Danny, Bryan, Oscar, and my Tio Miguel, to name a few. They are all black and brown men. Writing this book forced me to revisit their deaths. Some days were easier than others. This book is also dedicated to my brother-cousin, Poncho, who was killed five years ago. I think about you every day and I hope this book gets translated into Spanish so you can read this from wherever you're at. Thanks for always having my back when you were alive. This is also for his brother, my cousin Alberto, who has been incarcerated for the past ten years.

I want to acknowledge the death of Los Angeles rapper Nipsey Hussle, who was shot and killed outside of his store in South Central Los Angeles as I was making final edits to this book. I went to high school with Nipsey for a brief period of time and—like so many in L.A.—I was deeply affected by his death. It felt like we all lost a friend and a brother when we learned of his death. I hope I can continue to represent the city of L.A. like you did. The marathon continues.

Kendrick Lamar's album *Good Kid, M.A.A.D City* (*GKMC*) was either in my headphones or playing in my car throughout the entire book writing process. *GKMC* is the soundtrack to so many of our lives. And it was the album that I played the first time I drove to the cowboys' ranch and it hasn't stopped playing since. The album helped me understand the lives of the cowboys, the city of Compton, and myself in a much clearer way. I hope this book reads like that album continues to make us all feel.

Big shout-out to Cruzitas, one of the best cafes in the entire city. Thank you, Celina, Maria, and Lupita for creating such a positive environment for so many people in the community. And for reppin' Southeast L.A. at all times. I wrote so much of this book there and the love and light that I felt helped me through some of the tougher moments.

In addition to Cruzitas, I found myself writing this book on so many different airplanes, airports, and hotel rooms in different countries throughout the world while on assignment for the *New York Times*. I wrote from the Dominican Republic, New Zealand, Japan, England, Mexico, and Brazil, to name a few. Being away from Los Angeles and Compton helped me keep a bird's-eye perspective on the story.

I want to thank you for everything, Mama. I've been stealing and reading your books since you were a Ph.D. student in Literature at the University of California, Los Angeles (UCLA).

Your Chicana feminist books were some of the only books that I read growing up: Gloria Anzaldúa, Cherríe Moraga, and Sandra Cisneros, to name a few. How you managed to raise a badass boy on your own while in a Ph.D. program at twenty-five is something I will never fully understand. The day you decided to pursue work full-time because we needed money and not finish the program and pursue your own literary ambitions is something I think about often. You put my needs first and I'll never forget that. So, this book is for you and I hope I get to dedicate so many more to you, Mama.

My grandfather Walter Thompson was a prominent civil rights era *Oakland Tribune* staff writer and television and radio host. We met when I was twenty-five, almost two years after meeting my father. Meeting him for the first time and walking into his home, which was scattered with his old newspaper and magazine clippings, was one of the most memorable moments of my life. I dreamt that day, that one day I'd be able to do the same.

Lastly, I really want to thank the Los Angeles Unified School District (LAUSD) for my educational foundation. My classes were often under-resourced and we sometimes had to share books with two or three other students, but I wouldn't change a thing if I could do it all over again. I got expelled from four different high schools, went to a last-resort continuation school, and at one point I dropped out, not knowing what the future would hold. Kids like me were never told that we could become authors and journalists. But, shit, here we are.

This book is dedicated to the "black and brown kids in Compton" that Kendrick's mother, Paula Duckworth, refers to in a recorded phone call in the last section of "Real"—a song that is poignantly situated at the tail end of *Good Kid, M.A.A.D City*. I hope this book, like that album did, helps *change* some of the narratives in our world about black folks that aren't rooted in truth or love, forever.

ABOUT THE AUTHOR

WALTER THOMPSON-HERNÁNDEZ is a Los Angeles–based *New York Times* reporter and host. He is a part of a multimedia *Times* reporting team called "Surfacing" that covers subcultures, marginalized, and offbeat communities around the world. Before working at the *Times* he wrote for publications like NPR, *Fusion*, the *Guardian*, and *Remezcla*, among others. Walter has reported from every continent and throughout the United States. He attended the University of Portland, received his master's degree in Latin American Studies from Stanford University, and was enrolled in the UCLA Chicano Studies Ph.D. program for one year before leaving to write for the *Times* in 2018. Before graduate school, Walter played professional basketball throughout Latin America for three years.